Faculty Workload Studies
Perspectives, Needs, and Future Directions

by Katrina A. Meyer

ASHE-ERIC Higher Education Report Volume 26, Number 1

Prepared by

ERIC *HE*

ERIC Clearinghouse on Higher Education
The George Washington University
URL: www.gwu.edu/~eriche

In cooperation with

ASHE

D0108211

Association for the Study
of Higher Education
URL: http://www.tiger.coe.missouri.edu/~ashe

Published by

The
George
Washington
University
WASHINGTON DC

Graduate School of Education and Human Development
The George Washington University
URL: www.gwu.edu

Jonathan D. Fife, Series Editor

Cite as

Meyer, Katrina A. 1998. *Faculty Workload Studies: Perspectives, Needs, and Future Directions.* ASHE-ERIC Higher Education Report Volume 26, No. 1. Washington, D.C.: The George Washington University, Graduate School of Education and Human Development.

Library of Congress Catalog Card Number 98-84054
ISSN 0884-0040
ISBN 1-878380-81-8

Managing Editor: Lynne J. Scott
Manuscript Editor: Barbara Fishel/Editech
Cover Design by Michael David Brown, Inc., The Red Door
Gallery, Rockport, ME

The ERIC Clearinghouse on Higher Education invites individuals to submit proposals for writing monographs for the *ASHE-ERIC Higher Education Report* series. Proposals must include:

1. A detailed manuscript proposal of not more than five pages.
2. A chapter-by-chapter outline.
3. A 75-word summary to be used by several review committees for the initial screening and rating of each proposal.
4. A vita and a writing sample.

ERIC **Clearinghouse on Higher Education**
Graduate School of Education and Human Development
The George Washington University
One Dupont Circle, Suite 630
Washington, DC 20036-1183

> *The mission of the ERIC system is to improve American education by increasing and facilitating the use of educational research and information on practice in the activities of learning, teaching, educational decision making, and research, wherever and whenever these activities take place.*

This publication was prepared partially with funding from the Office of Educational Research and Improvement, U.S. Department of Education, under contract no. ED RR-93-002008. The opinions expressed in this report do not necessarily reflect the positions or policies of OERI or the Department.

EXECUTIVE SUMMARY

As states continue to be pressured to provide increased services with constrained resources, it should be helpful to
those in higher education—and in state legislatures and agencies—to understand the context within which the interest in
faculty workload developed and perhaps may be resolved.

What Conditions in the States Create
Interest in Faculty Workload?

Several trends are impacting states. Many states expect the
"baby boom echo" to hit higher education; at the same time,
more working adults need increased training and retraining.

The late 1980s saw faltering state and regional economies
and growing unemployment. States were asked to fund growing prison populations, K–12 enrollments, and individuals
needing social assistance. Rising taxes and stagnant wages
created an environment of growing public distrust of government, and some taxpayers revolted.

Concurrently, the costs of higher education rose as growth in
the HEPI exceeded growth in the CPI. Rising costs are caused
by several factors, including increases in fringe benefits, new
technology, more staff, and certain internal processes (Massy
and Zemsky 1992, 1994). To cover rising costs, parents and
students were asked to pay higher tuition.

Because the personnel budget often constitutes 80 to 90
percent of an institution's budget, state legislatures became
increasingly interested in ways to increase the productivity
of personnel. Studies of faculty workload were the result.

What Role Do Opinions Play in the Push
For Greater Faculty Productivity?

The business community has been a major critic of the quality and productivity of modern universities. Many legislators
view higher education as unproductive and unaccountable.
And the public is caught in a bind: Postsecondary education
is increasingly important for access to better jobs at the same
time increases in tuition are putting college out of reach.
Both sets of concerns increase the pressure to find ways to
improve productivity in higher education.

What Do Studies of Faculty Workload
Or Productivity Tell Us?

Over 15 states, several systems, and three national studies
have collected data on faculty workload. (These studies have

definitional problems and provide different answers, depending on the focus of the study.) While the majority of studies indicate that faculty work long hours—over 40 to 50 hours per week—the time spent in the classroom is usually much less. Time spent on teaching or teaching-related activities is larger, depending on the number of activities included in the definition. Percent of time spent on an activity provides another view of faculty's effort, and teaching usually exceeds all other activities. The few instances of longitudinal data or data from large-scale surveys (e.g., U.S. Dept. of Education 1990, 1995) indicate that time spent teaching has declined.

Studies of faculty productivity traditionally have looked at productivity in research, but few efforts have looked at (or defined) productivity in teaching and service. Many of these studies suffer from inconsistent or nonexistent definitions and a lack of trust in the measures that do exist.

What Beliefs Are Barriers to Finding Solutions To the "Productivity Problem"?

The focus on faculty workload is useful. It has not yet resulted in any gains in productivity, which may be because several beliefs keep us tied to increasingly questionable assumptions—that teaching equates with lecturing and that the classroom is the only place where learning occurs, for example. We also equate quality with inputs (e.g., full-time faculty, library holdings), and one input, time, is often used as an approximation of learning (although the belief that "seat time" and "credit hours" correlate to achievement is finding more critics).

We also tend to hold faculty responsible for all of higher education's problems and do not recognize growing competition from new educational providers. Those in higher education tend to believe that its current problems are not serious and that no major changes are needed. And this situation is compounded by a perceived lack of leadership. But finger pointing, excuses, and denials will not help higher education find an appropriate course into an uncertain future.

What Solutions Will Help Higher Education Successfully Engage the Future?

If continuing to focus on faculty workload does not appear to solve the productivity problem, then what might be more helpful? The first step is to let go, to become open to the unknown (Guskin 1996), for "we can't advance as long as we're holding tight to what no longer works" (p. 28). While the end may not be known, it will likely require a renewed focus on students' learning or encompass a shift from the old teaching paradigm to a new learning paradigm. Placing "students and their learning needs ahead of faculty preferences will have a profound impact on everything we now do" (Plater 1995, p. 24), which would drive changes in faculty work, institutional structures, and academic policies. Faculty will likely need to "not simply work harder at teaching but work smarter" (Edgerton 1993c, p. 6).

The focus on students' learning will require defining our outputs—skills and knowledge, competencies and level of proficiency expected—for courses and the baccalaureate degree. At the same time, new technologies will allow learning to occur at the time, place, and pace preferred by students rather than the institution. Technology can help improve productivity as well as make education available on every desktop.

To support these changes, institutions must adjust their missions to align more closely with public expectations, and the reward structure for faculty must be realigned to support teaching and a revised role for research.

The future is filled with dichotomies: increase quality and quantity of services *and* cut costs, standardize services *and* individualize programs, centralize *and* decentralize. But contradictions can create order by stirring things up "until, finally, things become so jumbled that we reorganize work at a new level of efficiency" (Wheatley 1992, p. 166).

Finding our way successfully to the future will require the minds, hearts, and emotions of all institutional members. Assumptions must be rethought, processes revised, behaviors relearned. We need to encourage creativity, restructuring, and experimentation if we are to discover what will work. And the entire community—as well as new leaders and fresh ideas—must be involved. At the same time, we will need to retain old values, such as service to others (Rice 1996).

Faculty must use their "smarts" to help devise the higher education institution of the future. Faculty will likely need to change their work to address students' learning, institutional priorities, and society's needs. But we will need all of their smarts to address the states' need for increased access, institutions' rising costs, and productivity.

CONTENTS

FOREWORD

Studies of faculty workload historically have been conducted for four basic reasons. The first, and most benign, reason is to gather statistical information about how faculty actually spend their time to understand the role of faculty. Second, faculty workload studies are funded by state legislators or boards of trustees because of a deeply held suspicion that faculty are not working very hard. Third, faculty have cooperated in workload studies because they believed that the data would demonstrate that they are working far harder than many think they are. And fourth, administrators need information on workload to make sounder management decisions.

Regardless of the reasons that motivated a particular faculty workload study, almost every study has had the same limitation: Data on how faculty spend their time are almost always gathered without consideration of the university's mission, the focus of a particular curriculum, and the career stage of individual faculty members. In other words, while faculty workload studies report on how the "average" faculty member spends his or her time, there is little contextual information that helps to make a judgment about whether or not faculty are spending their time appropriately and wisely.

A number of questions must be answered when developing faculty workload studies in the context of the process and outcomes of a particular higher education institution. What is the institution's overall mission and an individual school's or department's particular mission? How do individual faculty members spend their time in the aggregate for the department or school (compared with how faculty as an institutional average spend their time)? Are faculty spending their time consistent with the academic program's and the institution's missions? How can faculty workload studies better link how faculty spend their time with how well they actually spend their time? For example, what conclusions should be drawn from two workload studies where one reports that faculty spend 80 percent of their time teaching and the other that faculty spend 40 percent of their time teaching, while the graduation rate for the former institution is 40 percent of students and for the latter is 80 percent?

Faculty Workload Studies: Perspectives, Needs, and Future Directions, by Katrina A. Meyer, director of distance learning and technology for the University and Community College System of Nevada, examines in depth the purpose, results, and use of faculty workload studies. Dr. Meyer first sets the stage, examining motivation at the state level based on budget considerations and the general perception of increased demands for faculty workload studies. She then turns to a review of recent workload studies and their findings, and concludes the report with a review of concepts that appear to be barriers to improving workload studies and in-depth recommendations that would help to create more useful studies.

The usefulness of workload studies increases when they are more closely linked to process and outcomes. Data without context are mere numbers. Although they may be useful in supporting a particular ideology or political agenda, they are of limited use in furthering an understanding of the higher education enterprise. When placed in the context of process and outcomes, however, faculty workload studies can be a very positive tool in understanding how wisely faculty spend their time and whether an institution's policies and systems inhibit or support effective use of faculty time. The author has provided an integrative study that higher education leaders and policy makers will find useful as they work toward improving their understanding of the contributions that faculty make to their institutions.

Jonathan D. Fife
Series Editor,
Professor of Higher Education Administration, and
Director, ERIC Clearinghouse on Higher Education

THE SITUATION IN THE STATES

To understand the genesis of faculty workload studies in the states, we need to first understand the pressures placed on states by growing populations, faltering economies, rising costs in higher education, and taxpayers in revolt. It is in the context of these powerful pressures—more demands, fewer resources—that states' growing interest in seeing how faculty spend their time can best be understood. Ultimately, the issues are getting more out of the state funds going into the instructional budget and improving the productivity of faculty.

Population Pressures

Perhaps the easiest aspect of the future to understand is that the population will grow, and for many states, the numbers will grow dramatically. High school graduates nationwide—the "baby boom echo" or "Tidal Wave II"—are projected to reach 3.3 million by 2008, a growth of approximately 30 percent over 1992. The Western Interstate Commission for Higher Education (WICHE) prepares projections based on birth statistics and grade-by-grade enrollment data (WICHE 1993). The news is different in each region and state.

While all regions of the United States will see an increase, the West will experience the greatest growth in high school graduates, averaging from 45 percent growth in Oregon to 198 percent growth in Nevada. The eastern seaboard will experience growth averaging 20 percent in New England to 73 percent in Florida. The nation's midsection will see growth in the teens, except in Texas (39 percent), Colorado (36 percent), and Minnesota (35 percent).

Higher education planners across the nation are estimating how many of these high school graduates will arrive at higher education's door. Using conservative assumptions—that graduates will not change their current rates of going to college—forecasters predict a staggering number of recent high school graduates wanting to attend higher education institutions. Estimates suggest 455,000 new students by 2006 in California, over 120,000 new students by 2010 in Texas, 60,000 by 2010 in Washington State, 54,000 by 2015 in Arizona, 45,000 by 2010 in Florida, and 228,000 by 2005 in North Carolina. If we make traditional assumptions about how these new students will be served, these numbers appear to justify entire new institutions—new campuses, perhaps new systems—with capital costs in the billions. Based on "business-as-usual" per-student cost estimates, the California Higher Education Policy

Center (1996) projects that it will cost the state of California $5.2 billion to serve its 455,000 new students. To meet the demands of the growing undergraduate population, it has been suggested that California consider such alternatives as excluding all out-of-state undergraduates from public colleges, granting California financial aid to students who attend out-of-state colleges, ensuring full use of the accredited private institutions, prioritizing enrollments by age, and suspending graduate admissions to master's programs in arts and sciences at California State University campuses and to doctoral programs in the same fields at five University of California campuses (Breneman 1995).

These estimates are mostly conservative. It is likely that high school graduates' rate of attending college will increase as a result of several factors. First, graduates may pursue additional education as improvements in K–12 education both increase the number of high school graduates and improve graduates' skills. Second, graduates and their parents realize that a college degree is necessary preparation for entering many occupations, let alone qualifying for the growing number of jobs in the "knowledge industry." Third, college preparation has traditionally been justified as the road to higher earnings (see table 1); today, it may be the key to the sort of flexible skills and ability to learn new skills that will help ensure modest financial security. Some college, whether vocational training or a baccalaureate program, is no longer a luxury, but a requirement.

The demography lesson does not end here. Since 1950, the nation's population has become more diverse, from 10 percent nonwhite to 20 percent in 1990 (Pew 1995). African Americans currently make up 12 percent of the nation's total population, Asians and Pacific Islanders 3 percent, Native Americans, Eskimos, and Aleuts 1 percent, Hispanics 9 percent, and "others" 4 percent. In some states, minority populations account for a larger proportion of the state's population. And among the school-age populations that contribute to the growing number of high school graduates, minority youth will increase 4.4 million from 1990 to 2010 and account for 38.2 percent of all youth aged 0 to 17 in 2010 (Hodgkinson 1992).

In addition, many of the new students will come from lower- and middle-income families who will require some assistance to pay for college costs. Table 2 displays current information on the percent of first-year undergraduates needing financial assistance, from 56 percent in two-year public colleges to 74 percent in independent colleges (El-Khawas 1995). Further, most institutions estimate that at least 40 percent of their current undergraduates hold jobs during the school year (p. 25).

TABLE 1

Mean Annual Earnings by Level of Education, 1992

Level of Education	Mean Annual Earnings (Those 18 and Older)
Professional	$74,560
Doctorate	$54,904
Master's	$40,368
Bachelor's	$32,629
Associate's	$24,398
Some College	$19,666
High School Graduate	$18,737
Not a High School Graduate	$12,809

Source: U.S. Bureau of the Census, *Statistical Brief,* August 1994, cited in Rodriguez and Ruppert 1996.

Moreover, while the baby boom echo will involve increased numbers of traditional-age students, it is also true that current students in colleges and universities are different from the high school graduates seeking a residential college education of four or more years. In fact, the 5 million learners who enroll in community colleges are, on average, 24-year-olds with jobs and/or families. These students fit their education around work obligations, and despite their being termed "the emerging new majority," many traditional institutions have not adjusted their offerings to be attractive to this new—and growing—market.

Add to these factors the growth in the number of adults seeking retraining to change careers or to keep their current employment. While estimates vary, it has been suggested that every one in seven adults should be actively pursuing some additional training to stay abreast of requirements for their jobs. In a survey of businesses in Washington State, employers suggested that from one in four to one in five employees (depending on the industry) should be pursuing some additional training—which translates to millions of

TABLE 2

Percent of Students Needing Financial Aid, Fall 1994

Institutional Type	Average Percent of First-Year Undergraduates Needing Aid
Independent Colleges	74%
Independent Universities	67%
Public Comprehensive Institutions	62%
Public Doctoral Universities	58%
Two-Year Public Colleges	56%

Source: El-Khawas 1995.

adults nationwide desiring entry into higher education for a single course or for an entire degree program.

The numbers are staggering, and the implications are frightening. The cost of satisfying this onslaught of new students with "business-as-usual" approaches has attracted the attention of governors, legislators, and higher education leaders. Quite simply, the resources are not there to meet these pressures.

Faltering Economies

State economies are impacted by a number of forces: the general health of the nation's economy, the type of industries located within their borders, the play of markets and the actions of competitors, weather, international events, government actions, and the acumen of business leaders. In the early 1980s, the Midwest became the rust belt, impacted by the onslaught of attractive Japanese cars and massive layoffs in the auto industry. The mid-1980s brought an end to the cold war, and the "peace dividend" turned out to be layoffs at companies that had supplied materials and expertise to the military and a sharp increase in former military personnel looking for employment in an already constrained employment market. The 1980s and 1990s also brought dislocations in several natural resource industries, such as timber, fishing, and mining, that were affected by environmental regulations, harvesting and business practices, and competitiveness with other providers. And markets for products were no longer found only in another community or state but were increasingly found in other nations, and market competition became increasingly more international in scope.

Merger mania hit, and companies were bought and sold throughout the early 1990s. Signs of slowed economic growth can be seen in the annual growth in gross domestic product; the GDP grew modestly in most years, but growth was negative in 1974, 1975, 1980, 1982, and 1991. Productivity (in terms of output per hour) slowed; when indexed to 1992, productivity grew only to 101.9 by 1995. With debts to cover, downsizing and restructuring become popular tools to enhance lagging productivity. Unemployment reached 8.5 percent nationwide in 1975 and stayed around 7 percent through the 1980s. Recovery was uneven, and the recession affected some states and some industries more deeply and longer than others.

And for the first time, those finding themselves unemployed were not just blue-collar workers, but also managers and professionals. These individuals, more likely to hold a college degree, experienced an increase in unemployment rates from 1.9 percent in 1980 to 3.2 percent in 1993. (The unemployment rate for managers increased from 2.3 percent in 1990 to 2.7 percent in 1994.) The college-educated person expected to return to college to be retrained, to upgrade his or her skills, and/or to be trained for a new occupation.

States experienced these economic changes in several ways. First, state and local tax revenues fluctuated with the health of local economies, generally increasing but (more important) not keeping up with demand. Second, demand for a number of government services has increased. Prison inmates in federal and state facilities increased from 196,429 in 1970 to over 1 million in 1994. Enrollments in public and private K–12 schools increased from 46.2 million in 1970 to 49 million in 1993. Social security recipients increased from 35.6 million in 1980 to 42.2 million in 1993, supplemental security income recipients increased from 4.1 million in 1980 to 6.3 million in 1994, and families receiving Aid to Families with Dependent Children (AFDC) grew from 3.8 million in 1980 to 5 million in 1994. By 1992, federal social welfare expenditures had reached 12.4 percent of total GDP, and state and local expenditures reached 8.5 percent of GDP, up from lows in 1970 of 7.8 percent and 6.9 percent of GDP, respectively.

Third, to cover these increased services (as well as other types of services), taxes were taking a bigger bite out of family incomes. For state and local taxes only, a family of four earning $50,000 paid 8.8 percent of its income in taxes. The federal income tax rate for individuals earning $40,000

The cost of satisfying this onslaught of new students with "business-as-usual" approaches has attracted the attention of governors, legislators, and higher education leaders. Quite simply, the resources are not there to meet these pressures.

to $49,999 was 10.9 percent of adjusted gross income. Taxes increasingly were perceived as a drain on family resources.

Fourth, and perhaps most important, growth in per capita income has been stagnant. National data for the 1990s indicate that families in the United States have seen only a modest 4.3 percent increase in real per capita income, while the consumer price index increased 12 percent over the same time period (Washington Office 1996). Nationwide, the median household income began to decline in 1990, and by 1993 it had declined to a level below that of 1985 (U.S. Bureau of the Census 1995). Average hourly earnings (in constant dollars) actually declined from $7.78 in 1980 to $7.40 in 1995, with annual changes that were negative in 1987 through 1993 and in 1995. Median income for families (in 1994 dollars) also displayed stagnant growth, from $37,319 in 1976 to $38,782 in 1994. Families (of two or more persons) living in poverty increased over the same time period, from 9.4 percent in 1976 to 11.6 percent in 1994 (the percentages for African-American families living in poverty were 27.9 percent in 1976 and 27.3 percent in 1994). To put these data into perspective, median earnings totaled $22,205 for women and $30,854 for men in 1994. Coupled with rising taxes and other rising costs (such as for higher education), this situation created interest by taxpayers and legislators alike in pursuing tax cuts.

And more than "any other variable, the strength of the overall economy is what affects the level of higher education funding" (McGuinness and Ewell 1994, p. 3). Similarly, "worsening economic conditions reduce the discretionary income that students and their families need to pay tuition" (Waggaman 1991, p. 37). Therefore, future funding for public higher education institutions will continue to be heavily impacted by the health of the nation's and the host state's economy.

The Surge in Costs
This subsection reviews information on the rising costs of higher education and the sources of these rising costs, along with the type of costs and the values that encourage their growth. This discussion then leads into a review of the forces that many think have contributed to changes in the mission of higher education institutions. Last, it discusses tuition increases and the changes taking place in the proportion of higher education costs paid by students and government.

Sources of rising costs

The rising costs of higher education are well documented. Growth in the higher education price index (HEPI) exceeded that in the CPI by 20 percent from 1982 to 1995 (Research Associates 1995), and the annual increase in HEPI outpaced that in the CPI in every year with few exceptions (e.g., 1991). Salaries, fringe benefits, technology, new services and new staff, purchases and operations, work norms, and academic practices all contribute to the growing cost of higher education (see Waggaman 1991 for an excellent review). But many of these same factors affect business and government. What makes higher education different? Part of the answer can be found in higher education's experience with salaries, fringe benefits, new technologies, and growth in staff, but a large part of the answer can also be found in its norms and values and its labor-intensive practices.

Faculty salaries, after several sluggish years, saw three years of increases that outpaced inflation, but by only 1.4 percent overall (Magner 1996b). Information from the annual survey of the American Association of University Professors (1996) found that faculty, on average, earned $50,980 in 1995–96, which is highly variable based on the discipline, type of institution, and sector (public or private) one works in (see Research Associates of Washington 1996 for extensive data on these differences). Table 3 presents national data on average faculty salaries by rank for 1989–90 to 1994–95. Increases in administrators' salaries have also exceeded increases in inflation as well as the CPI (College and University 1996).

But it is in the area of fringe benefits—federally mandated benefits, health insurance, retirement payments—that increases have reached double digits. For example, a TIAA-CREF survey of 634 institutions in 1990 found that retirement and insurance plans totaled 21.1 percent of college payrolls (*Business Officer* 1991). The survey found that the average amount per employee was over $6,000 and that costs varied by type of institution and region. Mandated benefits averaged 6.6 percent of payroll, 5.9 percent of which was accounted for by increases in social security taxes. Pension and retirement plans averaged 8 percent of payroll, and insurance benefits totaled 6.5 percent, which included 6.1 percent for health insurance. The cost of health care has also been growing, by estimates ranging from 20 percent to 35 percent

TABLE 3

Average Salaries of Full-time Instructional Faculty, Current Dollars/Annual Change

Academic Year	Professor		Associate Professor		Assistant Professor	
1989–90	$52,810		$39,932		$32,689	
1990 91	$55,540	5.2%	$41,414	3.7%	$34,434	5.3%
1991–92	$57,433	3.4%	$42,929	3.7%	$35,745	3.8%
1992–93	$58,789	2.4%	$43,945	2.4%	$36,625	2.5%
1993–94	$60,649	3.2%	$45,278	3.0%	$37,630	2.7%
1994–95	$62,709	3.4%	$46,713	3.2%	$38,756	3.0%

Source: U.S. Dept. of Education 1996b, p. 1.

(Kramon 1991; Roush 1991), which generated greater federal and public review of health care in the intervening years.

During the 1990s, the demand for information services—computers, networks, telecommunications services—exploded. Institutions had to locate funding for new technologies, either through new state funds, reallocation of existing resources, fundraising, or innovative negotiations. Data on growth of Internet accounts and the use of Web sites tend to seem phenomenal—until the next set of data are published. The 1996 Campus Computing Survey (Green 1997) found that 67 percent of all undergraduates had access to e-mail and the Internet, 76 percent of all faculty also had Internet access, and 55 percent of the campuses surveyed had a Web presence. Use of e-mail in the classroom grew from 8 percent in 1994 to 25 percent in 1996.

Institutions have also seen growth in staff positions. Data for 1975 to 1985 show a 6 percent growth in faculty, 18 percent growth in "executive, administrative, and managerial employees," and 61 percent growth in "other professionals." Data for 1985 to 1990 show increases of 9 percent, 14 percent, and 28 percent, respectively (Grassmuck 1990, 1991). In the 1990s, the number of full-time professional staff grew 4.5 percent (Nicklin and Blumenstyk 1993), in contrast to increases in faculty of 1.2 percent and declines in all other staff groups, including administrators, clerical workers, and maintenance staff.

Part of the blame for this growth in professional staff can be laid at the feet of the new technologies, which require new staff to make them work and to help others learn how they can best be used. Part of the responsibility for increased numbers of professional staff has been the faculty's abdication of some responsibilities (advising, for example), and some responsibility must go to the needs of external and regulatory bodies. And part of the responsibility for the increase in professional staff is the growing heterogeneity of students enrolling in higher education. As minorities, the disabled, and other special populations with special needs enrolled in colleges and universities, new programs and support staff have been needed to ensure their eventual success at the institution (see Leslie and Rhoades 1995 for a review of the factors that appear to have increased administrative costs as well as some theoretical constructs for this growth).

To the extent that they need to purchase services, colleges are subject to paying the rising costs of the marketplace. Thus, they must pay increased prices for electricity, telecommunications, heating and cooling, snow removal, asbestos abatement, hazardous waste materials handling, and police and health services.

Some evidence suggests, however, that to the extent that some costs can be postponed, institutions do so. A recent study found that the average accumulated deferred maintenance on college facilities grew from $20.5 billion in 1988 to $26 billion in 1996 (Association of Higher 1996). Given that 60 percent of all college facilities were built more than 25 years ago, this problem will only increase, adding to the cost of higher education in the future.

Research Associates of Washington (in Pickens 1993) has tracked price changes for the major categories of expenditures (see table 4). The increase in prices from 1980 to 1992 ranges from a high of 167.08 percent for fringe benefits to a low of 39.47 percent for utilities (a regulated industry). The increase in costs of professional salaries (102.52 percent) and library acquisitions (138.87 percent) seems to contribute the most to exceeding the 97.55 percent increase in the HEPI for the same period. No study as yet has attributed the rising costs of higher education to each of these cost factors. While such a study would be useful, it would not necessarily explain the reasons for arriving at the current situation. For those reasons, we must understand the values that have encouraged these costs to rise.

TABLE 4

Measures of Price Changes for Various Expenditures in Higher Education, 1980–1992

	1980	1992	12-Year Increase
Professional Salaries	79.4	160.8	102.52%
Nonprofessional Salaries	80.2	140.4	75.06%
Fringe Benefits	72.6	193.9	167.08%
Services	76.5	144.6	89.02%
Supplies & Materials	84.6	118.1	39.60%
Equipment	81.6	125.9	54.29%
Library Acquisitions	79.5	189.9	138.87%
Utilities	64.1	89.4	39.47%
HEPI	77.5	153.1	97.55%

Source: Pickens 1993, p. 12.

The impact of higher education's values on costs

Work norms and academic practices bear examination for their roles in raising the cost of higher education as well. A number of illustrative terms help describe what is happening in higher education (Massy and Zemsky 1991, 1994; Zemsky and Massy 1990). "Academic ratchet" captures the steady shift of faculty allegiance away from the institution's goals toward those of the academic specialty. "Output creep" captures the faculty's swing away from teaching and toward research. The "ratchet" works through several processes, such as the pursuit of faculty "billets" or positions that add to the department's prestige even if enrollments are constant. Faculty members' "discretionary" time is increased as lower-cost staff and graduate assistants take over certain faculty functions, freeing faculty to perform more preferred activities, such as research.

Some evidence confirms the operation of the academic ratchet. Data from liberal arts colleges and research institutions were used to test whether departmental norms for teaching load, class size, and number of sections would act as the theory of the ratchet predicted (Massy and Zemsky 1992, 1994). Data on teaching load, for example, indicated that additional teaching loads are always viewed negatively.

The "administrative lattice" (Massy 1989; Massy and Zemsky 1991) posits the increase in administrative costs as a result of greater regulation, growing institutional complexity, a preference for managing by consensus, and the performance of functions formerly conducted by faculty (e.g., advising).

Further, the growth in number of administrators can result from the "accretion of unnecessary tasks," whereby staff perform tasks they enjoy although those tasks might not help the unit's productivity, and from "function lust," whereby problems are solved by hiring more staff.

Some authors have documented the "cost disease," whereby expenses grow faster than inflation, even when the number of staff and students does not change. The University of Delaware (Middaugh and Hollowell 1992) found that between 1985 and 1991, the CPI increased 24.8 percent but academic budgets increased 62 percent and administrative budgets increased 85 percent. As for the "administrative lattice," while the number of students enrolled increased 11.5 percent in the same time frame, faculty positions increased 14 percent, teaching or research assistant positions increased 20 percent, salaried staff increased 23 percent, and professional staff increased 48 percent. With regard to the "academic ratchet," teaching credit hours decreased 9.1 percent, class contact hours decreased 19.5 percent, and student credit hours per FTE faculty decreased 16.5 percent.

The work of Massy and Zemsky (1992) has also focused attention on the role of the proliferation of courses and increasing specialization in the growth of faculty and ultimately rising costs. "Destructuring the curriculum"—especially at the undergraduate level—has resulted in:

> . . . fewer required courses, less emphasis on taking courses in an ordered sequence, and greater reliance on students to develop their own sense of how the various bits and pieces of knowledge they acquire in the classroom fit together into a coherent picture (Massy and Zemsky 1992, p. 1).

"Destructuring" is a consequence of the faculty's pursuit of specialized knowledge or, in other words, their research interests. And pursuit of research is enabled through the workings of the "academic ratchet," which releases faculty from teaching duties to pursue individual interests.

Three other academic practices may play a role in raising the cost of higher education: sabbaticals, retirement, and tenure. The long-term academic practices of faculty sabbaticals and administrative leave have been questioned in some states (Lively 1994) and are increasingly under fire by cost-

The long-term academic practices of faculty sabbaticals and administrative leave have been questioned in some states (Lively 1994) and are increasingly under fire by cost-conscious state officials.

conscious state officials. The uncapping of retirement made it illegal to retire tenured faculty based solely on age, and current research (Bader 1995) notes that the median age at which faculty retire has risen, to just over age 65. Although this change in retirement age is unlikely to have a large impact on costs, it could have some modest impact.

Of these three academic practices, however, tenure is blamed for increasing the number of faculty who are permanently part of the institution's payroll. The percent of faculty who are tenured averages 57.6 percent at all institutions and is as high as 68.8 percent in public research institutions (U.S. Dept. of Education 1996a). Critics also focus on the role played by tenure in protecting the unproductive individual, thereby impacting the cost of higher education.

The "production functions" of higher education—the ability of institutions to make substitutions to improve productivity—can also play a role in higher costs; that is, higher education's "powerful norms" that govern faculty behavior create a "sticky" production process for teaching and learning (Zemsky and Massy 1995). Thus, the presumption is that the amount of inputs (number of faculty, number of hours taught) required to produce the outputs desired is fixed. To improve productivity, institutions may need to examine how learning is actually produced compared with how it is presumed to occur. They may also need to learn how to substitute technology for labor, thereby helping faculty reach more students (Massy and Zemsky 1995).

Higher education institutions are unique in several ways. Unlike commercial enterprises, their prestige, or pursuit of prestige, has traditionally been captured in terms of what was spent, not what is produced. Colleges have traditionally raised all they could and spent all they had, resulting in a situation where the cost of educating a student depended on the revenue available, not the necessary costs of producing an educated student (Bowen 1980). Prestige required new programs and new services, faculty "stars" and large, federal grants, the latest equipment, the biggest library collections, and the best facilities. Prestige required that an institution transform itself into a research institution, add graduate programs, and emphasize research and grantsmanship, resulting in the so-called "Carnegie creep." But prestige is not necessarily synonymous with quality (Pew 1992a). Prestige (defined as the ability to attract resources) is different from quality (the successful fulfillment of an institution's mission), yet most often, quality is defined as growth, especially in terms of revenue and/or expenditures.

A study of four selective colleges (Carleton College, University of Chicago, Duke University, and Harvard University) found that a large part of the increases in spending could not be attributed to market prices, faculty and staff compensation, financial aid, or administration (Clotfelter 1996). The study's author concluded that a "major culprit" was the institutions' "unbounded aspirations" to be "the best." (He also found that professors' teaching loads declined by 12 to 28 percent from 1977 to 1992, depending on the discipline.)

To be fair, however, others outside the institution also asked for increased services. Students asked for expanded placement assistance or intramural athletic facilities, communities lobbied for additional programs or services, businesses wanted to take advantage of research conducted by the faculty, and state governments asked institutions to provide assistance with economic development. In an effort to please, or perhaps to earn or retain a special place in the community, institutions found few needs that should not be met. The result has been a "muddling of mission that leads colleges and universities to be all things to all people, saying no to no one and, as a result, spawning enterprises that later gain autonomous life and power" (Pew 1991, p. 3A).

Given this background, there is no reason to expect higher education institutions to value lowering costs. Unless, of course, the level of revenues cannot support the pursuit of institutional goals. And that is what has happened.

The contribution of "mission confusion" to increased costs

The term "output creep" captures the process whereby faculty gradually replace teaching duties with research. It may involve hiring others (such as teaching assistants) to perform instructional duties, negotiating release time for research, or using external funds to buy release from instructional duties to conduct research. In any case, it is highly rational behavior for most faculty, who know—or are told—that the only way to succeed, to earn tenure and promotion, is to be a successful researcher or, more accurately, frequently published. Publishing—not necessarily research, although they are difficult to separate—is the key to personal gain and professional security, not teaching. "Publish or perish" may be an overused saying, but in many higher education institutions, it captures the facts as experienced by many faculty.

Evidence strongly suggests that the faculty's "research orientation" is negatively correlated with "student orientation" ($r = -.69$) (Astin 1993). Research orientation negatively correlates with several student-related variables, e.g., hours per week spent teaching and advising ($-.83$), commitment to student development ($-.72$), student orientation of the faculty ($-.69$), use of active learning ($-.52$), percent of resources invested in student services ($-.52$), and percent of faculty engaged in teaching general education courses ($-.52$). These values contrast with faculty "student orientation," which has positive correlations with hours per week spent teaching and advising ($.71$), faculty attitudes toward general education ($.64$), and faculty commitment to student development and social activism ($.60$), and negative correlations with use of graduate teaching assistants ($-.74$), average faculty salary ($-.64$), public university ($-.57$), and student/faculty ratio ($-.56$). These "contrasting patterns of correlations show that the tension between research and teaching in U.S. higher education is very real" (p. 411).

All of which is not to say that faculty and administrators agree with this situation. Most respondents to one survey, whether faculty, unit heads, deans, or administrators, felt that teaching and research ought to be of equal importance (Gray, Froh, and Diamond 1992). The reality, however, is that each felt research was overemphasized. If this outcome is true, why are the two not more balanced? The answer can be found in the results of another large study on teaching and faculty rewards (Fairweather 1992). Put simply, time spent teaching was negatively related to salary: Those spending 35 percent or less of their time teaching earned the highest average salary ($56,181), while those who spent 53 percent to 71 percent of their time on teaching and instruction earned an average of $37,244. Conversely, the average salary for faculty who had written only one refereed publication was $33,198, compared with an average of $56,183 for faculty with 30 or more refereed publications. These facts send powerful messages to faculty.

Moreover, the debate about rewards for teaching versus research is a reality (Fairweather 1993). Individuals who spend time on curricular reform cannot spend less time on research and expect to be rewarded under the current reward structure. "Faculty must make conscious choices between these activities rather than assuming that one simply reinforces the other. In the end, academe must confront the difficult trade-offs between teaching and research" (p. 47).

Three other molding forces should not be ignored. As doctoral students, individuals are enrolled mostly in research institutions and are inculcated with the research norms of their discipline—which explains some of the current attention paid to revising doctoral programs to encourage greater emphasis on pedagogy and valuing instructional duties (see Kennedy 1995). But professional and disciplinary associations also influence the goals and rewards available to faculty, and perhaps to a greater extent than the home institution.

Perhaps the greatest influence on the "mission drift" of institutions away from teaching and toward research, however, is the personal and professional goals of institutional leaders as well as faculty. Institutions, in and of themselves, do not seek to pursue different aims, but administrators and faculty can and do. To transform an institution into a research university with growing numbers of graduate programs and research grant dollars is the highest accomplishment toward which a new president can strive. Faculty value working with talented graduate students, and as faculty are also influenced by the rewards available to successful researchers, the drift upward in the Carnegie classification ladder is under way.

Yet the trend toward research has come under fire. Mostly, faculty are thought to be guilty if they pursue their own aims rather than those the public prefers, making a "mismatch between faculty priorities and the fundamental purposes of our institutions" (Rice 1996, p. 1) or a "disconnect" between higher education and the world (Pew 1996a). Some of what passes for research has been criticized by Senator William Proxmire in his annual "Golden Fleece" award for the most useless piece of federally funded research (Daly 1994). This type of faculty research has been disparaged as "scholarly drivel" (Schaefer 1990), "mediocre, expensive, and unnecessary" (Smith 1990), a "diversion" from real problems that reinforces the status quo (Fellman 1995), and "self-indulgent," a faculty "entitlement" regardless of the particular mission of the appointing institution (Pew 1996a, pp. 4–5). A somewhat less derisive description of the current type of research pursued notes that such research is of "low quality" and is "often inconsequential material, rather than the protracted pursuit necessary for a major intellectual contribution" (Mayhew, Ford, and Hubbard 1990, p. 131).

How have increased costs been covered?

Evidence suggests that the increased costs generated by these forces have been largely covered by students and the states. But their respective shares—the "balance of payments" if you will—have changed.

The share of institutional revenues coming from state and federal sources has declined. From FY 1980 to FY 1993, the distribution of funding sources for public institutions changed (see table 5). The federal government decreased its share by 12.7 percent, state governments by 21.3 percent. Institutions increased the share of funding sources coming from sales and services (up 19.4 percent) and tuition and fees (up 42.6 percent). In a survey of institutions, 56 percent and 58 percent of independent and public institutions, respectively, reported an increase in the share of costs paid by students and parents (El-Khawas 1995).

TABLE 5

Percent Change in Share of Total Revenues, FY 1980 versus FY 1993

Revenue Source	Public Institutions	Private Institutions
Sales and Service	19.4%	−0.4%
Tuition and Fees	42.6%	14.8%
Private Gifts, Contracts	53.8%	3.6%
Endowment Income	20.0%	−24.6%
Local Governments	5.3%	0.0%
Federal Government	−12.7%	−23.3%
State Governments	−21.3%	10.5%

Source: Breneman and Finney 1997.

This analysis begs two points. States have increased funding for public institutions by approximately 4 to 5 percent per year, or 45 percent from 1985–86 to 1995–96 (Hines and Higham 1996), but the growth in state funding has not kept pace with the rising costs generated by institutions (see also Pickens 1993). Therefore, although the distribution of funding support is changing, it has not necessarily occurred within an environment of active cost containment among institutions. In other words, states may continue to value higher education but may not be able to afford its unconstrained growth. The quandary: The public is increasingly skeptical that "the public and private price of [higher education] can be sustained—no matter how valued it may be" (Eaton 1995, p. 18).

Increases in tuition are also well documented. From 1991 to 1995, resident undergraduate tuition at public research institutions increased 41 percent (see table 6) (Breneman and Finney 1997), compared with a 12 percent increase in the CPI and a 4.3 percent increase in real per capita income during the same period (Washington Office 1996). It is no wonder that parents have begun to express their concern about continued increases in tuition to public officials and the national and local media are increasing their coverage of the issue.

Two additional issues are pertinent to the discussion of tuition. The first relates to who benefits and who should pay for this benefit. Traditionally, the benefits of public higher education have been seen to accrue to both the individual and the public; thus, paying for higher education was shared between the state and the student. But has the rising cost of higher education dictated a different answer to this question? The more relevant policy question is, Should it?

The second issue is whether the cost of tuition has risen above the means of average families and taxpayers to pay it, thereby putting higher education seemingly out of reach for their children. This situation would have sociological and political ramifications. As the traditional road to gaining access to professional employment and leadership, higher education has helped to improve equal opportunity for most able students. If its role is perceived to be closed to many citizens, the viability of higher education in the political arena will also be questioned.

Taxpayers' Revolt
The public, faced with an uncertain future, is understandably nervous. Citizens see rising taxes and government waste in the public sector, corporate mergers and downsizing in the private sector. Growth in per capita income has stagnated, and concern is growing that the once burgeoning middle class is beginning to shrink. Who is to blame? In a survey by Louis Harris and Associates (Vamos 1996), respondents mostly blamed government for their woes: 72 percent of respondents mentioned increased government spending, and 66 percent of respondents named high taxes. Private busi-

TABLE 6

**National Averages in Resident Undergraduate
Tuition by Institutional Type**

	1991	1992	1993	1994	1995	Total Percent Change
Universities	$2,156	$2,410	$2,627	$2,837	$3,032	
		+12%	+9%	+8%	+7%	+41%
State Colleges and Universities	$1,735	$1,940	$2,123	$2,277	$2,402	
		+12%	+9%	+7%	+6%	+39%
Community Colleges	$947	$1,052	$1,148	$1,231	$1,314	
		+11%	+9%	+7%	+7%	+39%
Private Four-Year Institutions	$9,391	$10,017	$10,498	$11,025	$11,709	
		+7%	+5%	+5%	+6%	+25%
U.S. CPI	+4.2%	+3.0%	+3.0%	+2.6%	+2.8%	+11.9%

Source: Breneman and Finney 1997.

ness came in for its share of criticism: 59 percent blamed their woes on the decline of the manufacturing economy, 52 percent blamed increasing global competition, and 46 percent blamed the excesses of big business and Wall Street. This pessimism affected their perception of their own and their children's future. Sixty-seven percent thought the American dream of equal opportunity, personal freedom, and social mobility was harder to achieve than in the previous 10 years. Fewer respondents thought their children would have a better life, and more thought their children's lives would be worse than was the case in 1989.

And how might this pessimism manifest itself? One likely outcome has been the growing number of limits on taxation and/or spending passed by state citizens. Twenty-eight states—over half—now have tax or spending limits in law; 12 of them have enacted constitutional limits on taxing and spending. Fifteen states' limitation laws are tied to growth in personal income, and many of these laws limit spending (not revenues), allowing for politically attractive tax rebates or refunds. To spend in excess of the established amount requires a "super"-majority vote of 60 percent of the legislature in 11 states.

For example, California approved Proposition 13 in 1978, which limited property taxes. Californians passed the Gann initiative, a spending limitation, in 1979 and Proposition 98 in 1988, which protected funding for K–12 education and junior colleges at 46 percent of annual state revenues. Michigan voters approved the Headlee Amendment in 1978 to limit tax revenues. In 1992, Florida passed a limit on increases in property taxes; it also has a constitutional amendment that restricts growth in state revenues to the five-year average increase in personal income. Massachusetts's Proposition 2½ and legislation in Nebraska limit increases in property taxes. In 1992, on the heels of a new personal income tax, Connecticut voters approved a constitutional amendment to cap state spending. South Carolina has seen cuts in property taxes, Kentucky limited increases in property taxes, and Texas passed a constitutional amendment that tied increases in state spending to growth in personal income. Arizona has a constitutional amendment that limits growth in appropriations to 7.12 percent of personal income and requires approval by two-thirds of the legislature to increase taxes. In 1979, Oregon citizens limited state spending to growth in personal income. In 1993, the citizens of Washington State passed Initiative 601 limiting the growth in state spending to the growth of inflation and the general population (this restriction does not affect the growth in revenues, which increasingly must be returned to citizens in the form of tax refunds). And in 1996, voters passed tax measures in California, Nevada, South Dakota, and Oklahoma.

Twenty-eight states—over half—now have tax or spending limits in law; 12 of them have enacted constitutional limits on taxing and spending.

Just what are the voters saying? The message has been variously interpreted as a directive to be more efficient, to curb government spending or the growth in spending, and to cut waste. The evidence from the states that experienced the first taxpayer revolts is clear: Higher education—along with other state services—will feel the pinch. But did voters mean to cut state spending or to curb taxes but hold higher education harmless? Or do voters see higher education as both contributor to and benefactor of increased state spending?

The Budget Squeeze
The resulting problem for states is fewer resources—or a cap on the growth of resources—at a time when costs are rising throughout the state budget. Table 7 documents the nominal and real (after subtracting inflation) increases in general fund state spending from 1979 to 1994. These numbers confirm that states experienced very minimal growth or declines in real terms in the early 1980s and early 1990s.

Spending for K–12 education, prisons, welfare, and medicaid, however, increased during the early 1990s (see table 8). In California, state spending on prisons grew by 25 percent in this period, while funding for higher education declined by 25 percent. Nationwide, however, state appropriations for higher education increased every year (except 1993), although spending could not cover the rising costs of operation. In 1995–96, state appropriations for higher education totaled $44.4 billion (Hines 1996).

In a study of six bellwether states (California, Connecticut, Florida, Massachusetts, Michigan, and Minnesota), higher education funding as a percent of the state general fund fell from 1990 to 1993 in every state except Michigan (see table 9) (Gold 1995). Over the same period, spending from the general fund on higher education declined in California, Connecticut, Florida, and Massachusetts in contrast to double-digit increases in K–12 education, welfare, medicaid, and prisons. Table 10 presents the percent change in state spending, by category, for the same six states, again showing higher education's losses in four states and modest increase in the United States at large.

This decline or slowing in state spending on higher education does not, however, present the whole picture. Federal spending on postsecondary education also declined 14 percent from 1980 to 1995 (National Center for Education 1995). Despite these declines, total revenues available to higher education institutions often increased because of increases in tuition and fees paid by students. A study of the California experience (Pickens 1995) documents trends similar to those nationwide. Tuition increased (or was charged for the first time at community colleges) to offset decreases in state appropriations. From the 1960s to 1990, instructional expenditures per student increased 444 percent at California State University and 413 percent at the California community colleges (p. 8). Adjusted for HEPI, however—which is heavily influenced by the cost of faculty salaries—the increase was 10.5 percent in the CSU system, and instructional expenditures per student decreased at the community colleges. This examination chronicles the dismantling of the California master plan that had guided the development of higher education in the state from the 1960s until the 1990s.

Yet this is not a simple case of "no resources, no funds." Some states, perhaps by reason of their priorities or political expediency, fund higher education despite the funding situation. Table 11 compares states whose one-year increase in appropriations for higher education were the highest and the lowest (Hines 1996). Even when the increase to the state's general fund (the state's *capacity* to spend) and its increase in appropriations (the state's *willingness* to spend)

TABLE 7
Nominal and Real General Fund Budget Increases, 1980 – 1994

Fiscal Year	Nominal Increase	Real Increase*
1994	5.1%	1.6%
1993	3.3%	−0.2%
1992	5.1%	1.5%
1991	4.5%	−0.1%
1990	6.4%	1.7%
1989	8.7%	3.5%
1988	7.0%	2.9%
1987	6.3%	2.6%
1986	8.9%	3.7%
1985	10.2%	4.6%
1984	8.0%	3.3%
1983	−0.7%	−6.3%
1982	6.4%	−1.1%
1981	16.3%	6.1%
1980	10.0%	−0.6%

*The state and local government implicit price deflator was used to determine real changes.
Source: Gold 1995, p. 24.

TABLE 8
State Spending Increases, 1991 – 1993

Category	1991	1992	1993
Total	5.2%	5.4%	4.6%
School Aid	7.1%	3.5%	3.0%
Higher Education	1.8%	0.5%	−1.5%
Corrections	9.2%	4.3%	6.9%
AFDC	9.0%	9.8%	4.9%
Medicaid	16.9%	19.6%	10.2%
Transportation	7.3%	2.6%	2.4%

Source: Gold 1995, p. 26.

TABLE 9

Composition of State General Fund Spending, by State, 1990 versus 1993

State/Year	K–12 Education	Higher Education	AFDC	Medicaid	Corrections	Other
California						
1990	37.8%	13.8%	5.5%	8.7%	6.1%	28.1%
1993	39.6%	11.8%	6.9%	13.1%	7.4%	21.3%
Connecticut						
1990	27.8%	7.0%	3.0%	8.1%	3.4%	50.7%
1993	22.8%	5.7%	3.1%	11.7%	4.6%	52.2%
Florida						
1990	50.0%	13.2%	1.4%	7.0%	6.1%	22.3%
1993	41.9%	11.8%	3.0%	13.1%	7.4%	22.8%
Massachusetts						
1990	19.6%	7.8%	3.9%	12.5%	4.4%	51.8%
1993	14.0%	4.7%	4.0%	14.5%	3.9%	58.9%
Michigan						
1990	29.9%	14.7%	5.4%	11.5%	7.6%	30.9%
1993	33.8%	15.5%	4.8%	13.7%	9.4%	22.7%
Minnesota						
1990	26.8%	19.9%	1.1%	10.6%	2.0%	39.6%
1993	28.8%	18.5%	2.0%	12.9%	2.3%	35.5%
United States						
1990	36.3%	14.0%	2.5%	9.1%	5.2%	32.8%
1993	36.5%	12.6%	2.8%	12.4%	5.7%	30.0%

Source: Gold 1995, p. 68.

TABLE 10

Percent Change in State Spending by Major Program Area, 1990 versus 1993

State	K–12 Education	Higher Education	AFDC	Medicaid	Corrections	All Programs
California	16.5%	−12.1%	19.0%	52.9%	24.4%	8.6%
Connecticut	12.3%	−15.4%	36.6%	64.3%	52.9%	15.1%
Florida	16.8%	−6.1%	101.1%	99.6%	29.2%	35.0%
Massachusetts	8.6%	−20.3%	34.9%	50.8%	14.1%	−2.0%
Michigan	32.3%	9.3%	0.9%	19.3%	22.9%	−0.9%
Minnesota	20.0%	2.0%	15.9%	45.1%	39.4%	18.9%
United States	22.1%	1.0%	23.8%	54.0%	22.2%	14.1%

Source: Gold 1995, p. 70.

were modest or nonexistent, some states found the funds for higher education. This finding belies, but does not substantially dispute, the words of one legislator, who claimed that "the most significant factor in whether we appropriate more money is if we have more money to appropriate" (Ruppert 1996, p. 31). Moreover, it is doubtful whether a state that is willing to spend money on higher education, regardless of its capacity, can sustain it over time in a highly charged political environment when other needs also inevitably grow.

The growth in appropriations for higher education has clearly slowed since the growth of the 1970s and 1980s (Hines 1996). For some states and institutions, the falloff in appropriations meant budgets would have to be cut. In 1992, for example, nearly 60 percent of the institutions responding to a survey by the American Council on Education had to cut their operating budgets for 1991–92 (El-Khawas 1992). By 1995, the situation had improved, with 63 percent of public two-year institutions and 82 percent of public four-year institutions reporting an increase in the budget (El-Khawas 1995). Table 12 presents this information for 1991 to 1995, capturing the "down" years of 1992 and 1993 as well as the improving conditions for 1994 and 1995.

The threat of further budget cuts is no longer simply a threat. Laws limiting taxes and spending combined with competing state priorities may make the threat a reality.

The Problem of Productivity
The pressures created by population growth, economic hard times, rising costs, taxpayers' revolts, and the resulting squeeze on state budgets from other services set the scene for states to ask higher education to improve productivity (see Layzell 1992). This "cost/quality/access collision" (Mingle 1992) is the inevitable clash of higher education's rising costs, traditional measures of quality that equate quality with higher costs, and the increasing demand for access.

And it is in addition to the public's growing understanding that higher education experiences a level of "wastage" that would be unacceptable in the private sector and to parents footing an increasing tuition bill. From 1977 to 1990, for example, the rate of freshmen graduating in four or fewer years decreased from 45.4 percent to 31.1 percent; during the same time period, the rate of graduation in six or fewer years also decreased, from 75.3 percent to 68.4 percent (U.S. Dept. of

Education 1993). And although increasing "time to degree" may be partly a function of the changing student clientele—more working adults and part-time students, for example—institutional practices come in for their share of blame.

Increasing attention is being paid to remedial education—essentially a rework of education provided in the K–12 system—and in the early 1990s, efforts in this area were under

TABLE 11

Comparisons of Revenue "Capacity," "Willingness," And Higher Education "Effort"

States	Increase in General Fund ("Capacity")	Increase in State Appropriations ("Willingness")	Increase in Higher Education Spending ("Effort")
Top Nine One-Year Gainers (FY95–96)			
Nevada	–8.4%	–12.3%	15.0%
Georgia	4.3%	4.5%	8.8%
New Jersey	3.7%	4.4%	8.7%
Oregon	–0.4%	10.4%	8.6%
West Virginia	2.3%	1.9%	7.7%
Florida	3.4%	3.2%	7.6%
Ohio	3.5%	5.5%	7.1%
Mississippi	0.0%	0.9%	6.9%
Missouri	4.3%	8.7%	6.8%
Mean in FY96	1.4%	3.0%	8.5%
Mean in FY95	5.1%	9.3%	12.9%
Mean in FY94	6.0%	9.1%	9.4%
Mean in FY93	7.8%	7.0%	8.4%
Bottom Nine One-Year Gainers (FY95–96)			
Alaska	–2.9%	–2.1%	0.4%
Tennessee	6.0%	5.1%	0.4%
Wyoming	1.3%	0.0%	0.1%
Connecticut	4.2%	5.0%	–0.1%
Montana	2.2%	5.0%	–0.6%
Wisconsin	5.4%	5.7%	–0.8%
New Hampshire	–11.0%	–12.0%	–2.5%
Alabama	4.1%	0.9%	–7.6%
New York	–0.1%	–2.1%	–9.3%
Mean in FY96	1.0%	0.6%	–2.2%
Mean in FY95	5.7%	2.8%	–1.3%
Mean in FY94	3.4%	1.7%	–5.1%
Mean in FY93	3.6%	1.6%	–4.6%

Source: Hines 1996, p. 8.

TABLE 12

Percent of Institutions with a Budget Increase Compared With the Previous Year, 1991–1995

Type of Institution	1991	1992	1993	1994	1995
Public Two-Year	80%	57%	55%	73%	63%
Public Four-Year	66%	52%	59%	75%	82%
Independent	85%	85%	79%	96%	95%

Source: El-Khawas 1995, p. 27.

way in 10 states (Lively 1993) as a way to reduce further waste in higher education. Thus, Louisiana must end remediation at four-year universities as a result of a federal desegregation order; West Virginia considered a "warranty" program whereby high schools would guarantee their graduates are ready for college; Arkansas and Tennessee considered reducing remediation courses; Oklahoma, Virginia, Texas, and the city and state systems of New York considered raising entrance requirements; and Nebraska and Washington undertook studies to assess the extent of remedial education in their institutions.

A third type of "waste," and perhaps the most troubling, is what the Wingspread Group (1993) calls the high cost of "weeding." The education system appears to be more "organized to discourage students—to weed them out—than it is to cultivate and support" (p. 5). This practice is the opposite of the current claim that "all children can learn." While higher education has traditionally certified individuals to perform essential tasks (and thus has an important role to ensure that unqualified individuals are not certified), the practice of "weeding" tends to leave many individuals who can learn— given a different method of delivery or more time or more assistance—without benefit of further education. (And although the charge to eliminate the waste of weeding *and* remedial education appears counterintuitive, it does focus attention on society's need for higher education to change its assumptions about whom it is to serve and how.)

But it is the cost of this benefit that is problematic. Figure 1, although a complicated chart, displays the several trends that capture the pressures on states, institutions, and families. While appropriations per FTE student rise and fall, rising tuition increasingly fills the gap created by higher education costs' rising faster than states can support. The family's share of total higher education funding consequently increases, and the "family payment effort"—tuition as a percent of median household income—experiences the steepest increase. This situation has enormous import for the political environment surrounding higher education as legislators and families question higher education's productivity and call for more efficient operations.

Where to focus attention? States have chosen to focus attention on faculty effort. Why? At between 80 percent and

FIGURE 1

National Trends in Constant Dollar (HEPI-Adjusted) Appropriations, Tuition, Total Funding, Family Share of Total Funding, State Payment Effort, and Family Payment Effort, 1977–78 to 1995–96

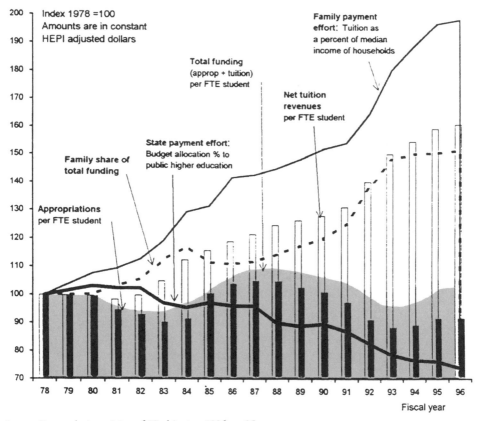

Source: Research Associates of Washington 1996, p. 35.

90 percent of many institutional budgets, the portion of the instructional budget devoted to personnel is likely to reap the greatest—and perhaps most immediate—benefits. And the vast majority of the instructional budget concerns faculty. It is not too far a leap to ask whether this substantial portion of the institutional budget can be more productive. This assumption is the genesis of the faculty workload/productivity studies that swept the states in the late 1980s and early 1990s.

All of these factors:

> . . . *converge on a single point—universities and colleges must become more effective managers of resources and redeploy faculty and staff time to meet needs more efficiently at a higher level of quality. [As] most other resources are fixed, faculty and staff time is the only resource that can be changed significantly to improve performance. Time becomes our most important fungible resource* (Plater 1995, p. 26).

In hindsight, this emphasis may have been, if not misplaced, then poorly focused. Before judging the studies, however, we will need to appreciate the perceptual realities surrounding the push for studies of workload and the studies themselves. Then it will be possible to evaluate what would contribute to a better understanding of, and solutions for, higher education's "productivity problem."

THE ROLE OF PERCEPTIONS

As if the economic pressures placed on states were not enough, legislators also hear negative comments about higher education from their constituents, many of them powerful businesspeople. Their perceptions are largely of an enterprise broken, not irretrievably, but damaged or costly or unresponsive. Some positive voices exist, of course, but they may seem self-serving or be dismissed or not believed. Increasingly, states' perceptions of higher education are colored by the growing belief that something needs fixing, somehow. The cry for studies of faculty workload is likely a symptom of the larger dissatisfaction with higher education.

How Business Views Higher Education

One can derive the business view of higher education from three sources: documents that business associations prepare to affect legislation or mold public opinion; the media's interviews with and articles about business leaders; and public forums about the future of higher education.

Without a doubt, business relies on higher education for much of its labor force, for the basic research or technological developments that it can parlay into a worthy product, and for the purchase of business services. But its criticism of higher education seems to be most virulent when it comes to the quality of future and current employees and when higher education is viewed as a consumer of public resources, such as the taxes businesses pay.

Some find the quality of current college graduates cause for concern. The 1993 National Adult Literacy Survey (NALS), for example, found that "only about one-half of four-year graduates are able to demonstrate intermediate levels of competence in each of the three areas [reading, writing, quantitative skills]" (cited in Plater 1995, p. 29). Moreover, 56.3 percent of American-born graduates of four-year colleges were unable consistently to perform such tasks as calculating the change from $3.00 after buying a 60-cent bowl of soup and a $1.95 sandwich (Wingspread 1993). Such inability would, of course, impact businesses immensely, either in terms of lost productivity or through the increased cost of providing the missing training themselves.

An American Imperative, prepared by 16 business and higher education leaders, claims a "dangerous mismatch" exists between what Americans need from higher education and what they are getting (Wingspread 1993). The report reviews the results of NALS and claims that there are too many graduates who "cannot read and write very well, too many whose intellectual depth and breadth are unimpressive, and too many whose skills are inadequate in the face of the demands of contemporary life" (p. 1). Further, "too much undergraduate education is little more than secondary school material—warmed over and reoffered at much higher expense, but not at correspondingly higher levels of effectiveness" (p. 7). The report urges institutions to tailor their programs and services to the needs of students, to publish explicit standards of entry and exit in terms of the knowledge, skills, and abilities that applicants and graduates will have, and to develop a required curriculum.

How Legislatures View Higher Education
Recent information from the National Conference of State Legislatures indicates that elected legislators are drawn primarily from the business sector and, to a lesser extent than perhaps was the norm in the past, the law. Since 1976, the percent of legislators who are attorneys declined from 22.3 percent to 15.5 percent in 1995. The percent of legislators who come from the business sector (including real estate)—business owners, executives/managers, business employees—also declined, from 30.8 percent in 1976 to 25.9 percent in 1995. It is not surprising that state legislatures often express concerns similar to those expressed by the business sector—except they now are in a position to make decisions about funding and policy.

A survey of higher education committee chairs and other influential legislators found that legislators' views of higher education are influenced by constituents' complaints and the media, with Republicans paying greater attention to the former and Democrats to the latter (Ruppert 1996). Personal experiences with higher education institutions—as students, parents, or in some other capacity—count for a great deal in forming opinions about higher education, as do value judgments, which are stronger than empirical evidence to the contrary. This finding is reminiscent of the caution that one should "never underestimate the difficulty of changing false beliefs by facts" (Rosovsky 1990, p. 259).

As a result of budget concerns, many legislatures have begun pushing for higher education to pay greater attention to state priorities. The highest priorities named in the survey of legislators (Ruppert 1996) were teacher preparation (mentioned by 88 percent of respondents), undergraduate education (86 percent), the improvement of K–12 education (82 percent), and job training and continuing education (79 percent); only 30 percent of respondents mentioned basic research. These results can be seen as an implicit criticism of—or at minimum a dissatisfaction with—higher education's current priorities as this group perceives them.

Legislators also have a "widely shared perception that the costs of higher education are increasing at a rate higher than other public enterprises" (Ruppert 1996, p. 24). In conjunction with the growing population of college-age students many states expect to face in the near future, legislators either "somewhat agree" or "strongly agree" that solutions to the crisis of access can be found in electronic technology (100 percent), routing more students through community colleges (71 percent), requiring faculty to teach more (67 percent), and shortening the time to degree (65 percent). A 1993 report by the National Center for Higher Education Management Systems (NCHEMS) found legislators' concerns were focused less on how hard faculty work than on students' access to specific required courses, senior and full-time faculty, small classes with opportunities for frequent feedback and active learning, computing resources, and preferred majors.

Republicans and Democrats view the sufficiency of funding for higher education differently. Republicans are more likely to think that current funding is adequate to meet current needs (63 percent), while only 26 percent of Democrats think so. When asked whether the current level of funding is adequate to meet future needs, Republicans are more optimistic (33 percent agree) than Democrats (18 percent agree). Thus, the balance of power in state legislatures—controlled by Democrats or Republicans—could affect the perception of adequate funding and the subsequent level of appropriations.

Legislators increasingly want to see the results of earlier appropriations, either in the form of reports on accountability, "report cards," or performance indicators. Some 34 states (Alaska, Arizona, Arkansas, California, Colorado, Connecticut, Florida, Georgia, Hawaii, Idaho, Illinois, Indiana, Kansas, Kentucky, Louisiana, Maryland, Massachusetts, Michigan, Minnesota, Missouri, New Jersey, New Mexico, New York, North Carolina, Ohio, Rhode Island, South Carolina, Tennessee, Texas, Utah, Virginia, Washington, West Virginia,

Wisconsin) now undertake some form of accountability reporting, either by the state, by an institution, or by the higher education system.

Forms of performance-based funding—that is, tying future funding to performance indicators or the attainment of goals—are in place or planned (in whole or in part) in 14 states (Arizona, Arkansas, Colorado, Connecticut, Florida, Idaho, Kentucky, Minnesota, Missouri, Nebraska, Ohio, South Carolina, Tennessee, and Texas) (see Layzell and Caruthers 1995), but approaches to performance-based funding are under discussion or have been partially implemented in many more states (including Massachusetts, New York, North Carolina, and Washington). It is likely that even more states are considering linking performance to funding, although they have not yet developed details on how to do so.

However highly they may value higher education, legislators listen to voters. And voters have been interpreted as saying that "other priorities must take precedence over higher education" (Ruppert 1996, p. 9). This stance, combined with budget shortages, has resulted in the fiscal situation discussed earlier.

How the Public Views Higher Education
What the general public thinks
Always difficult to capture, the "public" is easier to speak for than to actually find and survey. The "public"—although somewhat ill-defined, we all know who it is—perceives faculty as being unavailable to students, using aging lecture notes, and droning away to nearly empty lecture halls. Everyone has heard about—although no one knows who this fellow is—the faculty member mowing the lawn at midday, keeping irregular work hours, and ignoring social problems to pursue esoteric research projects. These stories may be apocryphal, but that makes them no less powerful in influencing public opinion about higher education.

But we need not rely solely on these stories to know what the public actually expects and thinks of higher education. At least for the general public of the 1990s, the work of Harvey and Associates (1994), Harvey and Immerwahr (1995a, 1995b), and Immerwahr and Harvey (1995) is illuminating. Although "higher education enjoys a huge reservoir of public goodwill" (Harvey and Immerwahr 1995b, p. 2), the public's knowledge of higher education is limited. Put simply, the public believes

The hypothesis is that this ignorance of higher education could mean that the public would not defend higher education from budget cuts.

that the primary purpose of going to college is to get a good job, the credential is more valuable than the education, the quality of the experience depends on a student's motivation, and colleges could be operated more efficiently. The hypothesis is that this ignorance of higher education could mean that the public would not defend higher education from budget cuts (Harvey and Associates 1994).

On the other hand, the public is deeply concerned about rising tuition. "'Sticker shock' is a real phenomenon in the public's mind, and the public believes that costs are escalating beyond the reach of the middle class" (Harvey and Immerwahr 1995b, p. iii). In fact, the "extent and depth of growing public anger about [rising tuition] is startling" (p. 13). Over 75 percent think tuition is overpriced and not a good value for the money; 65 percent worry that college is becoming too expensive for themselves or their children.

A similar survey of California residents found that Californians were increasingly anxious about their ability to afford college (Immerwahr and Farkas 1993). Over 75 percent of respondents felt that high school graduates should go to college "because in the long run, they'll have better job prospects," yet 52 percent did not believe that qualified students could go to college. They saw college prices as increasing faster than inflation (62 percent), leading 64 percent to support a "fundamental overhaul" of California's public college and university system. A follow-up survey four years later found that public anxiety had lessened somewhat, leading only 44 percent to support an overhaul of California's higher education system (California Higher Education 1997). But the public was consistent in its view of higher education's primary purpose: 79 percent (up from 75 percent) indicated that the most important goal of a college education is to give students "marketable skills."

And sometimes the worst critics of higher education are the disgruntled students who express their views to friends and family and the press. A history graduate, for example, wrote in the *Los Angeles Times* (June 17, 1991) about the "vast emptiness at the core of today's liberal arts education." These opinions of higher education may be the result of the "free-floating discontent" and cynicism of today's students (Atkinson and Tuzin 1992), who are "willing to believe that professors are lazy, self-centered, contemptuous of students, and abusers of the tenure system" (p. 27). Such attitudes in

A history graduate, for example, wrote in the Los Angeles Times *about the "vast emptiness at the core of today's liberal arts education."*

time become the "focused contempt of tomorrow's voters" (p. 27).

In 1995, a telephone survey of Washington State residents found that one-third of respondents said they wanted to pursue more education for themselves; some 20 percent of respondents were actually planning to return to school (Elway Research 1995). And of those planning to return to school, 92 percent thought they would be able to do so. For those with children, 91 percent expected their children to pursue education beyond high school; 71 percent thought a college degree was necessary in today's world. (In national surveys, 88 percent of Americans believe that a high school diploma is no longer enough to qualify for a well-paying job [Edgerton 1993c].) Another national survey found that 81 percent of those surveyed thought that getting additional education was important for them to be successful at work (Dillman, Christenson, Salant, and Warner 1995). Moreover, 50 percent of respondents aged 40–49 and 35 percent of respondents aged 18–39 indicated that their employers had encouraged them to seek additional training. These findings indicate that much of the public appreciates the need for additional education—for both themselves and their children.

Respondents to the Washington survey also indicated that a number of objectives were "somewhat important" or "very important": training or retraining workers for needed occupations (93 percent), helping residents reach their full potential (90 percent), creating a better quality of life in Washington State (89 percent), providing education in basic skills not learned earlier (88 percent), and helping the state develop its economy (87 percent). This information implies that the public is deeply interested in its own and the state's welfare—what Daniel Yankelovitch terms a shift from idealism to pragmatism (Edgerton 1993a)—and that higher education should also be deeply committed to the welfare of the public and its home state.

Last, 81 percent in Washington State thought that paying taxes in the state entitled them to access to public postsecondary education. This expectation is tempered by the public's growing pessimism: Yankelovitch found that 87 percent of Americans surveyed felt that college costs are "rising at a rate that will put college out of reach of ordinary people" and 79 percent felt that it is getting harder for average families to provide a college education for their children (Edgerton 1993a, p. 4). Americans, in other words, believe that college is "becoming more and more indispensable—and less and less within reach" (p. 4). This view presents a sobering problem for both legislators and higher education: If the public's need for higher education is denied, both elected officials and higher education institutions may feel the public's wrath.

What leaders think

A survey of various prominent "leaders" (many drawn from business) in California found that the leaders were extremely knowledgeable about higher education, much more so than the general public (Immerwahr and Boese 1995). In fact, those who know a lot about higher education think it should "solve its own financial problems before seeking more help from government" (Immerwahr and Harvey 1995, p. B2). In other words, higher education must "be prepared to make major changes to hold down escalating costs" (Immerwahr and Boese 1995, p. vii).

A similar comparison of the opinions of the public and community leaders found the two groups to be "polar opposites" in their understanding and evaluation of higher education's performance (Harvey and Immerwahr 1995a). Leaders were generally more critical about the "declining quality of graduates . . . the decaying utility and value of university research . . . low faculty productivity . . . general mismanagement . . . [and] higher education's financial problems, for which they show little sympathy" (p. 6). Faculty, viewed as "underpaid altruists" by the public, come in for their share of criticism from leaders for teaching too little and not working hard enough.

Many of the leaders interviewed in the California survey hold graduate degrees, and thus "the gap that long existed in the levels of educational attainment between academics versus other leaders has narrowed . . . if not totally disappeared" (Wadsworth 1995, p. 15). Leaders are less sympathetic about the current problems facing higher education and may be very critical. While the public worries about the cost of higher education to *its* families, leaders focus on the cost of higher education to the *state* and, ultimately, the taxpayers.

Real anger is directed toward higher education, and that anger comes "principally from the makers and shapers of public policy—governors, legislators, regulators, heads of public agencies" (Pew 1994, p. 6A). These individuals believe that colleges and universities "have become too isolated from the economic pressures that are forcing most other American enterprises to rethink purpose and mission, to reduce scope by scaling back the size of their operations" (p. 6A). There are two reasons for this anger: a lack of accountability for funding and the inability of many graduates to be "effective workers or informed citizens" (p. 6A). The anger is also directed at faculty, who "openly disdain the opinions of others . . . [and] who don't work hard enough anyway, [enjoying] not just greater job security but better pay than most taxpayers" (p. 6A).

The danger is that although higher education enjoys "genuine respect, affection, and goodwill" (Harvey and Immerwahr 1995a, p. 29), it is the purveyor of a "good"—the college credential—that is necessary for entry to higher-paying jobs. The public and its leaders will exert more and more pressure to increase access to this necessary good, and thus higher education will likely face increasing financial pressures as well as increasing regulatory pressures. Higher education's "best defense against the threat of regulatory intrusion is a convincing demonstration that it can live up to [its] promises" (p. 31).

How Higher Education Views Its World

Higher education—and the people within its institutions—do not speak with one voice, and both critics and defenders are making themselves heard.

Robert Zemsky is one critic who has been characterized as a practitioner of "tough love" for higher education, describing higher education as a "privileged class largely out of touch with the tough realities of the 1990s," "blithely unaware of what worries most Americans: job security, obtaining adequate health care, and securing a safe retirement," and "oblivious to just how much and how fast the world is changing" (Zemsky 1996, pp. 81–82).

Faculty groups are also making themselves heard. A joint statement prepared by a group of faculty leaders from New York and California attributes public criticism of faculty workloads to misunderstandings by "'outsiders' who do not appreciate how universities operate" (R. Wilson 1997, p. A12). The group blame governing boards and administrators if faculty do not work hard enough, as it is their responsibility to establish clear expectations and to evaluate professors accordingly. Faculty do support some changes in current practice, including initiating post-tenure reviews, reevaluating how they spend their time, and increasing the use of new technologies.

But it is Peter Ewell (1994b) who has best captured the type of miscommunication evident in current conversations between those who are outside higher education and those who are inside. He tells a story of a faculty person who pleads that "you need to make them (meaning the legislature) understand the damage they are doing," and later a legislator observes, "They still don't get it, do they?" (p. 80).

In this environment, much is not "gotten." Miscommunication—when the message is not heard from the speaker's point of view—is rampant in the exchanges of faculty and legislators. In fact, the worlds of faculty and legislators are not just different, but radically different. Faculty believe that legislators "won't give us the money we need (and we know you have)," yet legislators respond that they simply do not have the money. Faculty charge legislators with sacrificing "quality by doing more with less," yet legislators say that faculty need to change what they do. Faculty hear legislators claim that "faculty don't work hard enough," yet it is more likely that legislators mean that students are not getting what they need. Faculty hear legislators say they do not "trust faculty to do a good job, so we'll run higher education ourselves," yet legislators would really prefer higher education to take responsibility for what it does. Ewell argues that higher education needs to pay attention to what outsiders are saying without interpreting it as a personal attack or misinformed criticism, but as a sincere attempt to get higher education to attend to several serious problems.

Many insiders like to state that the United States is blessed with a higher education system that is the envy of the world. This statement, however, ignores that many believe higher education could do better and that having a vaulted reputation does not protect one from external scrutiny or prevent the need for constructive criticism. In other words, although higher education's contributions in the past cannot be ignored and should not be diminished, it does not mean higher education is perfect and can avoid making needed changes.

Two questions point out the different perspectives of higher education and its external constituents. The question most often asked within higher education is "How can society be made to recognize and support the value of what we

Taken together, the states' budget crises, higher education's own rising costs, and the growing perception of business, legislators, and the public that higher education needs to improve its productivity led inexorably to the first calls for studies of faculty workload.

do?" But the question most often asked by legislators, employers, parents, and students is "How can higher education serve us better?" (Pew 1996a, p. 9). This tension is exacerbated by the realization that many outside higher education already recognize and value what higher education does but that, as a society, we can no longer pay all of its bills. As for service, higher education believes that it serves the external world admirably, providing just the services it feels we need; the served, on the other hand, regard the current service to be less than adequate and want more and/or different services. Until the parties find some way to fully communicate and understand the opposing points of view, the cross-talk may continue, to everyone's ultimate frustration.

The Push for Faculty Workload Studies

Taken together, the states' budget crises, higher education's own rising costs, and the growing perception of business, legislators, and the public that higher education needs to improve its productivity led inexorably to the first calls for studies of faculty workload. This gathering of forces:

> . . . [is the] end to the public perception of the collegiate campus as a place of sanctuary, a place where values other than the purely financial might prevail. . . . Whatever their claims to a special calling, these institutions are no different, no better, no longer exempt from public scrutiny (Pew 1991, p. 6A).

At the same time, the public press produced a number of scathing books about higher education and, in particular, a greedy and lazy professoriat (e.g., D'Souza 1991; Huber 1992; Smith 1990; Sykes 1988). While those in higher education may not have read these publications, a growing number of critics who increasingly could be found among state legislators and the federal government did. The situation was ripe for state action, and, in response, several states undertook studies of faculty workload. The next section review the studies and their findings.

RECENT STUDIES AND THEIR RESULTS

States and systems that undertook studies of faculty workload or productivity often began such efforts in an ebullient spirit and finished in some discouragement. Studying what faculty do and produce involves many challenges, and changing what they do and produce is even more difficult. Suffice it to say that faculty workload was not the solution to the states' need for improved productivity from its institutions, but it would require a number of faculty workload studies to make it clear.

Studies of Faculty Workload
Definitions of faculty workload
Faculty workload is commonly defined as time spent on professionally appropriate activities, although in other contexts, a faculty member would refer to "workload" as duties assigned or completed. Time is a constrained resource, as a day has only so many hours for fulfilling one's personal, family, and career obligations. Thus, the focus on faculty time may not be a suitable substitute for a measure of productivity, but it does capture the choices made by—and implicit values of—faculty in allocating this precious resource.

Three measures of interest are usually used to assess faculty workload. First is the total number of hours faculty work per week in the fulfillment of their current jobs. Second—of interest to legislators—is the number of hours spent each week teaching or on instruction-related activities. Actual teaching is usually specifically defined as that time spent in the classroom, which is a subset of all related instructional activities, defined as preparing for class, correcting papers, grading, advising, and even research related to preparing classroom lectures or assignments. Third is the number of hours spent each week on research or other scholarly activities. Sometimes this information is reported in terms of hours, at other times as percent of total effort. In any case, studies of faculty workload vary substantially by state and institution, yet they yield largely similar results. (Some states, such as Texas, have defined "workload" in terms of semester credit hours generated, which may be more appropriately termed a measure of productivity.)

Several caveats about faculty workload are in order, however, before reviewing these studies. Different studies use different definitions for similar terms (teaching may mean only direct classroom instruction in one study but include several support activities in another), so direct comparisons of results are not possible. NCHEMS has worked on the design of a national database with common definitions of terms, which will go far toward solving some of the problems with current studies and data. But this design is not yet in place, so current data will have to suffice. It is also important to understand that these studies used different methods of collecting data: some from self-reports and others from an administrative database, some that used a sample of faculty and others that used all faculty, some using one-time data and others using longitudinal information. (For a thorough review of research methodologies and cautions, see Yuker 1984.) These conditions could place in question any one set of results, but they could also make consistencies even more interesting, given the disparity between studies.

Review of state studies

Numerous studies have collected data on faculty effort. At least three major efforts to collect data have been national in scope (Astin, Korn, and Dey 1991; U.S. Dept. of Education 1990, 1995). Since 1990, over 15 states and a number of systems have completed studies of faculty workload. (Individual institutions or systems might also have completed studies, but those studies are not included in this review.) The appendix contains an annotated list of these studies. While the majority of studies occurred in the late 1980s and early 1990s, reporting requirements continue to keep faculty workload on the legislative agendas of many states.

Study findings

Table 13 presents the data on total hours spent per week on all activities. Whatever the type of institution, faculty seem to work over 40 hours per week at their jobs and often exceed 50 hours per week. The figures decline substantially, however, when the measure is hours spent in the classroom (see table 14). While the figures vary by institutional mission, state, and year, the national data from the U.S. Department of Education (1991) average a low of 6.6 hours per week at research institutions, eight hours at doctoral institutions, and 10.5 hours at comprehensive institutions. The figures increase substantially when the measure is percent of time spent on instructional activities (see table 15), variously defined. While the definition likely impacts "percent of time," faculty appear to

TABLE 13

Total Hours per Week Spent in All Activities

Type of Institution	Total Hours Worked per Week
Public Research	57
Private Research	56
Public Doctoral	55
Private Doctoral	53
Public Comprehensive	52
Private Comprehensive	51
Liberal Arts	52
Public Two-Year	47

Source: U.S. Dept. of Education 1991, using fall 1987 data.

TABLE 14

Average Weekly Classroom Hours

State (Year of Report)	Institutional Mission	Average Weekly Classroom Hours
U.S. Dept. of Education	Research	6.6
(1991, using 1987 data)	Doctoral	8.0
	Comprehensive	10.5
California State University (1990)	Comprehensive	11.0
Virginia (1991)	Research/Doctoral	10.0
	Comprehensive	13.0
Arizona (1992)	Research	8.2
	Doctoral	12.4
Minnesota (1992)	Research	9.9
	State Universities	11.0
Washington (1994)	Research	7.1
	Comprehensive	10.7

Source: U.S. Dept. of Education 1991, using fall 1987 data.

spend half or more of their time on various instructional activities.

One of the few longitudinal studies of faculty workload surveyed faculty at DePaul University in 1986 and 1992, and found that the percent of time devoted to teaching and preparing courses declined (from 48.2 percent to 46.7 percent). Further, the faculty thought it desirable to spend even less time on these activities, or 38.7 percent of their time. While data from the U.S. Department of Education (1990, 1995) are not longitudinal, the findings indicate that the percent of time faculty spent on teaching-related activities declined from 56 percent in fall 1987 to 54.3 percent in fall 1992.

TABLE 15

Percent Effort on Instruction

Study (Year of Report)	Percent of Effort on Instruction	Instruction Includes:
SUNY (1990)	52.6%	Teaching and preparation
Rhode Island (1985)	76.0%	"Instructional matters"
Montana (1990)	47.3%	Instruction, course development, advising
California State University (1990)	61.1%	Teaching, advising, paperwork
U.S. Dept. of Education (1991, using 1987 data)	56.0%	Teaching, advising, supervising students, grading, preparing classes, developing curricula
U.S. Dept. of Education (1995, using 1992 data)	54.3%	Teaching, advising, supervising students, grading, preparing classes, developing curricula

These data, however difficult to compare precisely, allow a few modest conclusions. First, faculty members' effort on instruction or instruction-related activities varies by institutional mission (see table 16). Generally, faculty at two-year colleges teach more (or expend a greater percent of their time on instructional matters) than faculty at liberal arts institutions, who teach more than faculty at comprehensive institutions, who teach more than faculty at research/doctoral institutions. The differences in percent of time spent teaching by faculty rank are less striking (table 16) but can be characterized by full professors' allocating a smaller percent of time to teaching activities than associate professors, who spend less time teaching than assistant professors, who spend less time teaching than instructors or other faculty types. Last, the time spent on research/scholarship activities (see table 17) is also different by institutional mission, with faculty at research institutions spending more of their time on research activities (approximately 30 percent) than faculty at other types of institutions, with faculty at liberal arts and two-year colleges spending 8 percent and 3 percent of their time on research, respectively.

TABLE 16

Percent of Time Spent on Teaching by Institutional Mission and Faculty Rank

	Percent Effort
By Type of Institution	
Public Research	43%
Private Research	40%
Public Doctoral	47%
Private Doctoral	39%
Public Comprehensive	62%
Private Comprehensive	62%
Liberal Arts	65%
Public Two-Year	71%
By Faculty Rank	
Professor	51%
Associate Professor	53%
Assistant Professor	56%
Instructor	68%

Source: U.S. Dept. of Education 1990.

In 1989–90, a nationwide survey of faculty was used to develop a set of national norms based on then-existing patterns of faculty work (Astin, Korn, and Dey 1991). These norms, which provided a basis against which results from state studies could be compared (see table 18), revealed that half the professoriat in public universities and four-year colleges taught five to eight hours or nine to twelve hours per week, respectively. Further, approximately half of the professoriat at both types of institutions spent five to twelve hours per week preparing for teaching but only one to four hours per week advising students. On the other hand, two-thirds of the professoriat spent one to four hours per week on committees, and three-fourths of the professoriat spent fewer than

TABLE 17

**Percent of Time Spent on Research by
Institutional Mission**

Type of Institution	Percent Effort
Public Research	29%
Private Research	30%
Public Doctoral	22%
Private Doctoral	27%
Public Comprehensive	11%
Private Comprehensive	9%
Liberal Arts	8%
Public Two-Year	3%

Note: Research is defined as "research, scholarship, and creative works;
preparing or reviewing articles and books; attending or preparing for professional meetings or conferences; writing proposals; attending workshops
or conferences" (U.S. Dept. of Education 1990).
Source: U.S. Dept. of Education 1990.

four hours per week on administrative duties. Research and
scholarly writing showed greater variability among institutional
types, however; one-third of the faculty at public four-year
colleges spent one to four hours per week on research, but
faculty at public universities were evenly distributed across
several time categories. These figures help to put the results
from the separate state studies into context and to confirm
that, despite a number of questions about methodologies used
in these studies, their results seem to be in line with the national norms.

Conclusions from state studies

If one common conclusion can be drawn from these studies, it
is that faculty work long hours. In fact, a body of research documents the stress experienced by faculty caused by the demands of both work and family (Dey 1994; Dua 1994; Gmelch,
Lovrich, and Wilke 1984) or by being overextended, with too
many interesting projects or obligations (Hampel 1995).

Undoubtedly, the vast majority of faculty work hard at their
jobs, as currently designed. The question is whether they are
spending their time on activities that reflect institutional and
state priorities. Many states would answer that they are not. In
terms of state responses, however, studies of faculty workload
have resulted in few legislative actions. In Ohio, for example,
the legislature mandated a 10 percent increase in undergradu-

ate teaching. In West Virginia, the legislature demanded that faculty productivity exceed the average faculty productivity of similar institutions by 10 percent. In Florida, the legislature passed the 12-hour rule: "Each full-time equivalent teaching faculty member at a university who is paid wholly from state funds shall teach a minimum of 12 classroom contact hours per week." (Exceptions could be granted for other assignments, however.) In Maryland, legislative language directed the number of courses to be taught, which differed according to campus mission. In Colorado, institutions adopted policies requiring faculty to spend 30 hours per week (at Colorado State) or 40 percent of their time (at the University of Colorado) on teaching and teaching-related activities.

The majority of legislative responses have involved initiating, continuing, or expanding the requirement to report faculty members' instructional effort. A survey prepared for the State Higher Education Executive Officers (SHEEO) found that 21 states had some mandate for minimum faculty workload or for the reporting of faculty workload (see table 19) (Hauke 1994). The majority of states require reporting of instructional effort, perhaps in an attempt to focus attention on an activity it wants to increase. An update on state activities found that the number of states requiring reports of faculty effort rose to 23.

One can interpret this lack of legislative action in two ways. Either legislatures are loathe to legislate in this area, or they are hopeful that with continued legislative pressure—such as through the requirement of reporting—institutions will address productivity issues on their own, and with better results. Legislatures may be aware that workload is a complex and highly charged issue and that a simple, legislatively mandated solution will therefore not work. Their patience may be short-lived and the need to have institutions actively work on appropriate changes ever more essential, however.

Studies of Faculty Productivity
Definitions of faculty productivity
One might conclude, perhaps correctly, that the real question hiding behind the effort to understand how faculty spend their time is how productive faculty are. The two words—workload and productivity—should not be confused, although they are commonly used interchangeably. Workload traditionally captures how time is spent, while productivity is a measure of

Either legislatures are loathe to legislate in this area, or they are hopeful that with continued legislative pressure—such as through the requirement of reporting—institutions will address productivity issues on their own ...

TABLE 18

National Norms for Percent of Faculty Effort

Hours per Week	All Institutions	Public Universities	Public 4-Year Colleges	Public 2-Year Colleges
Scheduled Teaching				
None	0.3	0.6	0.2	0.2
1–4	7.2	12.2	5.0	2.2
5–8	26.2	47.7	19.6	5.1
9–12	32.0	27.1	45.0	14.8
13–16	17.6	6.6	18.6	31.6
17–20	10.1	4.0	7.6	25.9
21–34	5.9	1.6	3.3	18.5
35–44	0.5	0.1	0.5	1.5
45 or More	0.1	0.0	0.1	0.3
Preparation for Teaching				
None	0.3	0.5	0.2	0.3
1–4	8.4	10.4	7.5	8.4
5–8	22.9	26.0	22.1	22.6
9–12	25.2	25.9	24.9	26.0
13–16	17.3	16.7	17.1	17.3
17–20	13.8	11.5	15.2	13.9
21–34	9.4	7.3	10.0	8.9
35–44	2.0	1.1	2.2	1.9
45 or More	0.7	0.6	0.7	0.7
Advising/Counseling Students				
None	2.6	3.2	2.7	2.9
1–4	56.6	59.3	52.4	58.9
5–8	29.5	27.8	31.4	28.1
9–12	8.0	6.8	9.5	6.7
13–16	2.0	1.5	2.6	1.6
17–20	0.9	0.9	0.8	0.9
21–34	0.4	0.4	0.3	0.7
35–44	0.1	0.0	0.1	0.2
45 or More	0.0	0.0	0.0	0.0

what is produced with that time. Faculty note, quite correctly, that the percent of time spent on select activities or the number of hours spent in the classroom is not a valid measure of their productivity (Cooper and Hensley 1993). One can work long hours and be unproductive, and one can be extremely productive with modest expenditures of time. The confusion with regard to terms may be exacerbated by the lack of measures of productivity, giving rise to the predilection to use

Committee Work/Meetings				
None	4.6	4.6	3.1	6.5
1–4	68.6	63.8	66.0	75.3
5–8	20.6	24.1	23.9	14.3
9–12	4.3	5.4	5.3	2.7
13–16	1.1	1.5	1.2	0.8
17–20	0.3	0.5	0.4	0.4
21–34	0.1	0.1	0.2	0.1
35–44	0.0	0.0	0.0	0.0
45 or More	0.0	0.0	0.0	0.0
Other Administration				
None	36.5	36.1	37.0	41.2
1–4	38.6	40.4	37.0	37.3
5–8	11.5	11.2	11.0	10.7
9–12	5.8	5.4	5.9	4.8
13–16	3.0	2.6	3.5	2.5
17–20	2.3	2.2	2.8	1.6
21–34	1.7	1.5	2.2	1.5
35–44	0.4	0.5	0.3	0.3
45 or More	0.2	0.1	0.3	0.2
Research/Scholarly Writing				
None	20.2	5.4	13.5	51.6
1–4	27.9	17.7	33.3	31.6
5–8	15.4	17.0	19.8	9.5
9–12	12.4	18.3	13.7	4.2
13–16	7.3	11.6	7.8	1.2
17–20	6.7	12.2	5.9	1.1
21–34	6.3	12.4	4.6	0.5
35–44	1.8	3.5	0.9	0.1
45 or More	1.0	2.0	0.5	0.2

Source: Astin, Korn, and Dey 1991.

measures of workload, however dubitable they may be. Until good measures of productivity are available, it is not likely that the focus on workload will wane.

Despite these caveats, the two words share some characteristics. Both are difficult to define, and both suffer from changing values: What was valued in terms of what was produced in the past may not be what is valued today.

Our understanding of productivity

Faculty productivity has traditionally been defined as "research productivity," or the number of publications produced in a

TABLE 19

States with Mandates to Report Faculty Workload

No Mandate (27)	Mandate from Higher Education Authority (7)	Mandate from State Legislature (17)
Alabama	Arizona	Arizona
Alaska	Illinois	Connecticut
Arkansas	Iowa	Florida
California	Mississippi	Indiana
Colorado	Oregon	Kentucky
Delaware	Rhode Island	Louisiana
Georgia	Wisconsin	Maryland
Hawaii		Massachusetts
Idaho		Minnesota
Kansas		New Mexico
Maine		Ohio
Michigan		Pennsylvania
Missouri		South Carolina
Montana		Texas
Nebraska		Utah
Nevada		Washington
New Hampshire		West Virginia
New Jersey		
New York		
North Carolina		
North Dakota		
Oklahoma		
South Dakota		
Tennessee		
Vermont		
Virginia		
Wyoming		

Sources: Hauke 1994; Hines and Higham 1996.

year or a lifetime. This area of study has a long and creditable history (see Creswell 1985 for a review). We know, for instance, that faculty research productivity is tied to institutional mission, the environment of the host department, the availability of research-oriented colleagues, training in a tradition of research as a graduate student, and spending time on research activities (Bentley and Blackburn 1990; Blackburn and Lawrence 1995; Hekelman, Zyzanski, and Flocke 1995). Moreover, some evidence suggests the existence of "stratification" or, more colloquially, an "invisible college" that influences the publication of scientists trained at or working in influential institutions (McNamee and Willis 1994). That study of publication patterns in leading journals of chemistry, economics, philosophy, and sociology between 1960 and 1985 indicates that only a few prestigious academic institutions were represented in the journals studied.

A study of faculty productivity—defined as publications—and pay found the relationship was stronger in departments with strong norms emphasizing research and disciplines with scientific paradigms (Konrad and Pfeffer 1990). In another study of faculty productivity—again defined as publications—and cost, new faculty and higher-cost faculty explained 62 percent of the variance in production of publications (Noble, Cryns, and Laury 1992). These studies tend to support the truism that research is more prevalent, supported, and rewarded in institutions that emphasize it, more particularly in research and doctoral institutions, and that it is performed by young scholars and the more experienced faculty who have found success and/or personal reward in its performance. But as others noted in the earlier section on the dismal condition of much current research, this is productivity defined as numerical analysis, with the quality of the research presumed by having reached publication in a peer-reviewed journal.

Some attempt has been made to investigate the assertion that being a good researcher complements a faculty member's teaching ability. A sample of over 4,000 faculty from a variety of institutions found that faculty in the social sciences were the only group where consistent though modest relationships existed between the number of published articles and an instructor's effectiveness (Centra 1983). Nor did it find support for a "general ability" factor, with the conclusion that the relationship between performance in the two areas is either nonexistent or too modest to conclude that one enhances the other (Centra 1983). A later study that discussed common causes of research and teaching skills such as academic rank, general ability, personality, and amount of time spent on research found, on average, a very small positive association between research productivity and teaching effectiveness, as assessed by students (Feldman 1987). In any case, it would appear that the issue of whether pursuit of an active research agenda enhances teaching effectiveness must continue to be studied. In the meantime, the belief that research enhances teaching seems a powerful one.

...faculty in the social sciences were the only group where consistent though modest relationships existed between the number of published articles and an instructor's effectiveness.

But if research productivity at least has a methodology, teaching productivity has little discernable literature *or* methodology. In fact, the struggle to develop measures of productivity related to an institution's instructional mission has been difficult because of a lack of understanding of the outcomes of teaching in any other means than student credit hours or degrees granted. Both, one would hope, may stand in for students' actual learning, but neither is directly tied to the amount or quality of students' learning.

Instead, the emerging emphasis on teaching has focused on the development and refinement of the "teaching portfolio," about which research and evaluation studies are becoming available (see Centra 1994; Murray 1995). The portfolio, and other forms of assessing how well faculty teach such as peer review of teaching, should provide a means to evaluate the quality of teaching and may, with some thoughtfulness, tackle the question of its productivity as well. Further research on teachers' competencies (e.g., Smith and Simpson 1995) and evaluation of teaching using a talent development model (e.g., Sadowski and Hess 1994) will help build a base of knowledge with which to better understand a teacher's excellence and productivity. In the meantime, it should be remembered that no consensus currently exists about what constitutes high-quality teaching (Blackburn and Lawrence 1995).

A way to assess productivity as it relates to that portion of a faculty member's assignment called "service" is also needed. In one survey, faculty were asked their definitions of public service, generally defined as using faculty expertise to address societal needs for the benefit of the public (Schomberg and Farmer 1994). Service has been defined as "work that draws upon one's professional expertise and is an outgrowth of one's academic discipline. In fact, it is composed of . . . teaching and research but directed toward a different audience" (Elman 1994, p. 72). Regional accreditation processes could be a valuable means for changing existing methods of faculty evaluation (Elman 1994)—and perhaps workloads and rewards, as well. We will need to pay attention to developing appropriate measures—whether quantitative or qualitative—that help capture the variants of public service for the various disciplines and what "productive" service might be.

As productivity in teaching and service is defined, some of the lessons from the extensive literature on research productivity should be remembered. We know that productivity in research can be different for faculty from different groups, more particularly for minorities and women (see Konrad 1991). Moreover, we must expect productivity to wax and wane as faculty careers mature, talents are developed, and individuals adjust to different needs and family circumstances. Productivity cannot be linear, and it may take different forms over time.

Last, interviews with faculty underscored their professionalism and their commitment to "be the best they can be" (Massy and Wilger 1995, p. 19). Faculty care about their productivity but characterize it as maximizing research and publications. They are as efficient and effective as possible, and many work long hours, but the demands of research often mean that teaching is "satisficed" (doing enough to meet a standard of quality). And faculty view productivity as synonymous with results, not the ratio of outputs to inputs, as an economist would. Thus, improving productivity for these faculty means increasing outputs rather than producing the same or greater output at lower cost. These findings confirm that faculty do care about productivity and work hard to produce it, but that they value research productivity highly and instructional productivity to a lesser extent.

Problems with Workload and Productivity
As might be obvious, the current focus on faculty workload and productivity has numerous problems. Measures of workload can capture only *how* faculty time is spent, not how *well* it is spent. Faculty do not regard measures of workload with confidence, nor do they often comprehend the real concerns hiding behind the focus on contact hours. Thus, current measures of workload tend to capture how faculty work has been described traditionally (e.g., teaching, research, service) and not what states might prefer to result from the efforts of faculty. Legislators for their part rarely articulate the need to focus more on students, instead talking about faculty's "spending more time in the classroom." When studies reveal that faculty spend a small number of hours in the classroom, the normal legislator is appalled, and no amount of explaining about the many hours spent on other activities appears to change this opinion.

Moreover, measures of productivity have yet to be developed in any area except for research productivity. And even in this area, the chosen measure does not evaluate the quality of the research produced, except to rely on peer review as the harbinger of quality research. Ways to capture productivity in teaching and service are an important, yet missing, component of measuring productivity.

"Productivity problems are often rooted in a confusion about the ultimate objective [of higher education] and a lack of clarity about the ultimate customer" (Heydinger and Simsek 1992, p. 15)—true of both workload and productivity. None of our current measures of workload or productivity are clear about the ultimate objective and customer: Where is the student to be found in "hours spent teaching" and "number of publications per year"?

But one cannot hope for a change in focus away from faculty workload and productivity. A recent report urged colleges and universities to define and measure faculty productivity (Commission on National Investment 1997). Until better measures and better approaches are developed for gathering, understanding, and interpreting information about what faculty do and how well they do it, however, current measures of workload and productivity will likely be retained. They are both symptom and cause of our inability to analyze accurately the real problems that face us.

The last two sections attempt to provide a greater focus on issues relating to productivity. The next one discusses barriers to change, and the final one presents a number of approaches that have greater potential for improving productivity and performance in higher education than the current focus on faculty workload.

BELIEFS AS BARRIERS TO SOLUTIONS

If focusing on faculty workload is not a useful solution to higher education's problem of productivity, what is? And if states are serious about encouraging institutions to improve productivity, what would be a more useful focus? But before answers to these questions can be made clear, it is important to ask what other barriers exist to improving faculty or institutional productivity. For in the identification of barriers, possible solutions cannot be far behind.

Perhaps the line from the "Pogo" cartoon strip has been overused, but it is apt in our situation, and so we will use it again: "We have met the enemy and he is us." The enemy is within us, and it is the assumptions, beliefs, and traditions that limit our ability to think differently. This section presents an overview of several beliefs that are so common as to be truths, so ingrown as to be permanent. But these beliefs are neither truths nor permanent. And they must be seen for what they are if we are to go beyond them, to solutions.

The Teaching Paradigm

The fallacy many operate under is that teaching equates with lecturing and that the classroom is the only place where learning occurs. Both beliefs are dangerous in that they will likely impede our ability to redesign a very different type of higher education in the future. And this belief is not the province of faculty alone: It is held by many legislators who think that regulating contact hours or time spent by faculty in the classroom will actually have an effect on the quality or amount of students' learning.

We know that the traditional lecture is ineffective, and now, with the advent of technologies that allow students' access to education on a large scale, the lecture may be inefficient as well. It presumes that information may be passed from one person to the next by mere telling, which ignores current research on students' learning styles, the importance of active learning, and what information is. Information is not static but dynamic; it is not "content"—as in the content of education to be passed from teacher to student—but it provides "order . . . prompts growth . . . [and] defines what is alive" (Wheatley 1992, p. 102).

Moreover, teaching often occurs with no sign that students have learned anything as a result. In fact, higher education has often emphasized its elite function by placing the responsibility for learning on the student, allowing faculty to say "I taught, but they did not learn."

We must "move away from the concept of instruction as inextricably linked to hours in class" (Brinkman 1992, p. 29). We know that students learn more from their peers than from their interactions with faculty (Astin 1993). This belief will be difficult to give up, as it is most prevalent among those who have assumed that the only valuable learning (that which higher education promotes and certifies) occurs in classrooms, not in such environments as the workplace or from life experiences.

The gains in productivity resulting from information technology will be limited by the "view that learning occurs only when student and teacher are together in a classroom" (Brinkman 1992, p. 29). The tradition of "teaching as talking" and "learning as listening" contributes to a "sticky" production function that holds our conception of what level of productivity is possible to the current productivity of traditional instruction (Zemsky and Massy 1995). Faculty are reluctant to view technology as a way to substitute capital for labor and thus improve the productivity of students' learning (Massy and Zemsky 1995); with a "sticky" view of the production of learning, technology will be an "add-on" cost and will not help institutions improve productivity. Evidence of the "sticky" function of our current teaching assumptions is that when student enrollments are varied, the number of faculty vary closely, indicating that universities actually have very similar assumptions about the productivity of the faculty/student relationship (Olson 1994).

The classroom lecture tends to encourage the perception that faculty are the penultimate experts and that students are best advised to sit passively and take notes that capture the views of the person behind the lectern. Given the rapid expansion of information made available through the Internet, faculty increasingly recognize that they cannot, and need not, be experts in a field.

Further, teachers who lecture, albeit in a most impressive and stimulating manner, are still practicing active learning only for themselves; students tend to receive their words mostly passively. The traditional lecture tends to keep both faculty and students in bondage to a model of education that will serve neither particularly well in the future.

Measuring Inputs

It is a truism of measurement that we measure what we can, not what we ought. Afterward, our measures take on the patina of respectability, of capturing important relationships whether they do so or not. In the past, higher education has been prone to define quality in terms of a number of inputs— the number of full-time faculty, the number of books in the library, the number of students in a class, for example. These items can be easily counted and are sufficiently reasonable to seem to stand for some sort of quality.

We have measured such time-related inputs as credit hours, the number of weeks in a semester, and the amount of contact between students and faculty, and we have taken them for some sign of quality. The Carnegie course unit—a proxy for measuring students' learning—presumes that one learns "in proportion as one sits in the presence of a faculty member for 15-week periods" (Pew 1992a, p. 6A). Once again, these things are easier to measure than what all the credit hours and all the weeks in all the semesters were designed to promote—students' learning.

Of course, faculty have traditionally had the responsibility for assessing whether students have met the course's objectives and for grading their performance. While this system has worked well for many years, it is increasingly under attack by disgruntled employers who want to know what graduates know and are able to do and by members of the public who see college graduates who do not appear to possess college-level skills. (And in an environment of constrained resources, asking how much the state or individual is getting for its appropriation or tuition is increasingly likely.) It is not simply a case of questioning faculty judgment, but of seeking some sort of external validation of those judgments in terms employers can understand and taxpayers can see.

But "can measures of learning be devised that are readily understood and accepted both within the academy and in society generally? What troubles those who pose [this question] is the academy's insistence that measurement is next to impossible" (Pew 1996a, p. 4). Measurement may clearly be difficult, but solving difficult problems is the sine qua non of many able researchers. The claim that measurement is impossible does not ring true; it sounds peevish.

I refuse to believe that a community that has learned how to measure the distance to the farthest galaxies and to predict the outcomes of elections before they occur can deem it impossible to determine the quality and quantity of its own principle products (Langenberg 1992, p. 11).

The Tyranny of Time

We currently believe that time spent is some close approximation of learning acquired. It is not the "time-on-task" that researchers find correlates to achievement. It is, however, the presumption that credit hours, contact hours, quarters, and semesters are the only blocks of time within which students may learn (see O'Banion 1995). These concepts of time are tyrannous, because they mold our current structures in ways that are convenient for the organization, and are comfortable and known for those within the organization, but may be inadequate for students.

Much of the reform of the K–12 system has been an attempt to move the system away from "seat time" and "Carnegie units" toward focusing on students' learning. These time units did not vary even though learning varied, but we are moving now toward a system where learning is held constant and time will vary.

The Problematic Faculty

Two aspects of faculty life are important to remember. First, while many in the external environment view faculty as highly autonomous, faculty may have little actual power over such areas as contact hour requirements, registration systems, classroom assignments, equipment purchases and assignment for use, accreditation standards, budgeting, and the deployment of resources. Second, the provision of a modern education is a highly cooperative venture, depending on the joint efforts of other faculty, administrators, staff, librarians and student service personnel, food and housing services, ground crews, and protective services. Faculty do not act alone in the effort to educate students.

Therefore, focusing on individual faculty as change agents may not be sufficient—which is not to say that individual faculty are powerless or poor leaders, for the reverse is true. Two examples, however, illustrate the point. The National

Science Foundation spent millions of dollars on awards to individual faculty members to improve individual courses at individual institutions. In the 1980s, IBM spent additional millions funding more than 3,000 individual faculty projects. While both agencies meant well, neither program achieved results beyond the individual classroom. Clearly, making change in an individual classroom benefits the students within it, and thus these efforts are not failures. But both agencies intended their efforts to be more wide-ranging.

These examples illustrate two points. First, the predilection to blame faculty for everything wrong in higher education may be both misplaced and short-sighted, for it is neither true nor conducive to encouraging collaboration on appropriate solutions. Faculty make attractive targets, and increasingly "others blame faculty members for the real or perceived shortcomings of our colleges" (Lovett 1995, p. B2). But targeting all faculty with the qualities exhibited by only a few or blaming the entire profession for all the problems experienced by their institutions is not the way to encourage collaborative problem solving.

Rather than make one member responsible for everything, perhaps everyone needs to feel responsible for the success of the entire enterprise.

Second, faculty are partners in a system, and it is well to remember that systems comprise interconnected and interdependent parts, each part affecting others in ways that are sometimes difficult to predict. Faculty are not alone responsible for everything that takes place in an institution; they play a significant role, but so do all the other members of the organization—administrators, staff, and students. Rather than make one member responsible for everything, perhaps everyone needs to feel responsible for the success of the entire enterprise.

Market Competition

The perception has been that higher education has had a near-monopoly on the provision of postsecondary education and of widely accepted credentials. With the increase in potential educational customers, the emerging Information Superhighway, and businesses' growing dissatisfaction with the quality of our graduates, however, has come the development of a new market for educational services and the means for satisfying those new needs and customers. "Unfettered by the traditions of the academy," these new providers are preparing services and materials that appeal to learners—young and old alike—who are "accustomed to 'shopping' for the services they seek" (Pew 1996a, p. 3). Postsecondary education is making the transition to a commodity rather than a public good.

Some of these new educational providers will be created by for-profit entities, and others—such as the IBM Global Campus and the Western Governors University—will use existing courses and services from traditional institutions that are appropriate for distance delivery. "Virtual" universities will continue to proliferate as this new market evolves and new entrants attempt to capture a niche within it.

If higher education does not recognize that it will face unprecedented competition—not from a traditional four-year college but from an entity held together by a Web site—it will not adjust to the market and will lose its vaulted position. Such a situation could lead to a sense that traditional institutions are incapable of providing services required by students and parents, leading ultimately to questions about the viability of some institutions and ultimately to their possible demise.

Old Contentions and the Tactics of Opposition

As a society, Americans are known for their litigiousness and willingness to fight for their beliefs, illustrated in the following examples included in "Academe Today," a daily report produced by *The Chronicle of Higher Education* (November 19, 1996):

- Seventeen tenured faculty sue the University of Southern California over the decision to slash faculty salaries.
- Faculty at Southern Illinois University at Carbondale have voted to form a union.
- Teaching assistants strike at the University of California.
- Teaching assistants try to form a union at Yale University.
- Republican leaders in Congress announce their intent to examine the rising costs of attending college.

While these actions are the right of each group—and may be needed—they demonstrate our predilection for confrontation and old ways of handling long-standing contentions.

If the problems facing higher education are serious, and affect us all, we may not be able to afford to indulge in our usual ways of handling differences. It will require enormous courage to lay down our accustomed legalistic weaponry and confrontational tactics and engage in new ways of resolving problems. If we do not, however, our old contentions will surely be tomorrow's contentions.

The Seriousness of the Situation

Higher education has faced difficulties before and survived. To some, the problems facing states and institutions reviewed earlier are not serious, just an aberration that can be solved by waiting for better times to return, that in fact, there are no problems in higher education that cannot be solved by additional funding, from states or students, whichever is more likely.

Unfortunately, higher education cannot "hope for a cyclical upturn that restores funding to previous levels" (Pew 1996a, p. 5). Some sort of self-examination and redirection seems in order, if only the seriousness of the situation can be made clear. Like in the movie *Apollo 13*, higher education is getting too many phone calls conveying the same message: "We've got a problem" (Pew 1996b).

Those outside higher education, especially legislators, worry that "if left to its own devices, the academy would address change largely by remaining the same" (Pew 1996a, p. 4). Yet this course will likely result in the worst outcomes: waning public support and waxing criticism.

A Lack of Leadership

What normally happens when problems arise? We deny their reality, ignore the danger signs, increase revenues instead of cutting costs, put off the problem (perhaps through some creative accounting), and then cut back as painlessly as possible (Dunn 1992). Budgets are frozen, across-the-board cuts implemented, retirees not replaced, equipment budgets slashed, and maintenance deferred. These incremental actions provide us with the illusion of action but may actually prevent our engaging in serious consideration of real solutions. Presidents and academic leaders spend "too much energy and time on ameliorating symptoms instead of addressing the root causes of what is ailing higher education" (Lovett 1995, p. B1). The typical reaction is to "look for someone else to blame" and to point fingers at others ("those stingy legislators and alumni, those tenured faculty members who resist change, those underprepared students, . . . that incompetent president and her bureaucrats") rather than working together to solve core problems (p. B1).

What normally happens when problems arise? We deny their reality, ignore the danger signs, increase revenues instead of cutting costs, put off the problem (perhaps through some creative accounting), and then cut back as painlessly as possible.

We react, "offer rebuttals, make excuses, get defensive" (Myers 1993, p. 5). Administrators, charged by faculty to protect them from external demands, are increasingly in the role of the messenger who gets shot (Pew 1996b).

Leadership is a dangerous endeavor, because no one applauds the bringer of bad news—which may explain the paucity of leadership. This situation is unfortunate because we desperately need individuals with the heart and will to tackle the tough problems facing us today and move us toward tomorrow's version of higher education.

But words will not be enough. They will be useful in understanding the problem and forming a vision of the future, but actions—perhaps even bold ones—will be needed in short order. Solutions will result from beliefs different from those outlined in this section and the will to act on them.

USEFUL SOLUTIONS

This section focuses on what changes might be more conducive to improving productivity than continuing the states' emphasis on studying what faculty do or regulating faculty workload. These solutions—and more and better ones may arise as experience with these areas grows—appear to offer higher education institutions new tools, new frameworks, and new assumptions with which to ask the difficult questions about what they can do differently and how. States also need to examine their own assumptions and align their actions with the solutions that might actually bring about the improvements desired.

These solutions draw heavily from the proposed shift from teaching to learning (see Barr and Tagg 1995) and the restructuring that higher education must undergo to remain viable in the coming Knowledge Age (see Dolence and Norris 1995). The next century, so nearly upon us, will likely bring new challenges and new opportunities. The first step is to realize that much of higher education's world has changed and to begin understanding—to the extent it is known—how it can transform itself to succeed in its new world.

Let Go

The key to restructuring higher education is to start the process (Guskin 1996). We do not need to have a finished plan in place before beginning, nor do we need to have all questions answered before one step can be taken. In fact, possible solutions for the higher education crisis that is upon us call for the knowledge that:

> *Transformation of any sort—whether human or chemical or corporate—is a perilous passage at best, calling for a radical letting go, and an openness to the unknown. It's hard to imagine anything more frightening. And it's hard to find a more likely route to progress—for in letting go of the old form, we create the space for a new form that will work even better. It comes down simply to this: that we can't advance as long as we're holding tight to what no longer works. And we have to break the mold before a new form can emerge* (Marjorie Kelly, cited in Guskin 1996, p. 28).

Similarly, while the "problem is the system," saying that "systemic change" is needed does not "tell us what the content of that change should be" (Marchese 1995, p. 4). We know what should change, but we are less clear about what it should be changed to, for "you can't see the end from the beginning" (Norris 1996b, p. 8). But we must begin the journey, and most writers would agree that focusing on students is the place to begin the process.

Focus on Students' Learning

The most important adjustment may be to change our focus from teaching to learning. Learning should be "the basic business of any college" (Scott 1993, p. 5), but it does not mean focusing on teaching, which actually emphasizes the "privileges and perquisites of faculty." By focusing on learning, "we turn attention to the needs of students and society" (p. 5). Doing so will include reconsidering assumptions about teaching and learning and seriously exploring the changes in faculty work, institutional structures, and academic policies that a focus on students' learning would require.

This reexamination of assumptions has been described as a shift from a teaching paradigm to a learning paradigm (Barr and Tagg 1995). Such a shift will require a monumental change in perceptions and expectations, a change that will require rethinking administrative structures, instructional processes, and faculty roles. In the teaching paradigm, colleges *provide instruction;* in the learning paradigm, colleges *produce learning.* The shift captures a change in focus from one on means to one on ends. The implications of this change in mission are far-reaching and will likely cause enormous havoc and discomfort for those firmly ensconced in the old traditions; nevertheless, it is this difficult movement to the new paradigm—which is not new to many—that can revive and renew the higher education enterprise. In the days ahead, more writers like Boggs (1995–96) and O'Banion (1995–96) will continue work on what the new paradigm means, what it will look like when it is implemented, and what it can produce for students and their institutions of higher learning.

Many other writers have stressed the need to focus on students' learning. The focus, they say, should be changed to productivity in learning and higher education's "productivity problem" recast to be "insufficient learning," not excessive costs (Johnstone 1993, 1996). The culprits of insufficient learning are:

1. Excessive drift and aimless academic exploration, with academic schedules too often geared to the personal convenience of the teacher or the student;
2. Excessive nonlearning time resulting from vacations and poor use of the entire learning day;
3. Unproductive learning that results from an inability to focus on studies;
4. Insufficient use of self-paced learning; and
5. Insufficient use of college-level learning during high school (Johnstone 1996, pp. 1–2).

Productive learning, then, would involve reversing these conditions to:

1. Maximize learning per unit of instructional resource (e.g., teaching time);
2. Minimize the downtime in student learning;
3. Reduce aimless curricular exploration;
4. Maximize potential college-level learning during the last years in high school;
5. Help students acquire better study habits and lessen some of the distractions of jobs, athletics, or socializing; and
6. Better individualize the pace of students' learning (e.g., through the expanded use of technology) (Johnstone 1996, p. 2).

"Academic departments [should] more closely match faculty interests and capabilities with [students'] needs and learning" and place "more responsibility on students themselves" (McGuinness and Ewell 1994, p. 1). The first directive focuses on the institution's responsibility to maximize students' learning through whatever means necessary, the second on students' responsibility to make their time spent at the institution as valuable and efficient as possible. Clearly, we will need *both* institutional change and greater responsibility on students to affect productivity in learning.

Moreover, "placing students and their learning needs ahead of faculty preferences will have a profound impact on everything we now do" (Plater 1995, p. 24). In the past, faculty assumed that they knew students' needs and objectives better than the students themselves. While "there is truth in this premise," it is "not enough for faculty to ignore students' own definition of need" (p. 24). This change will require an entirely different relationship with students, one that puts their needs at the center of the enterprise.

And this change has a number of implications for faculty: Their role will be increasingly defined in terms of their ability to facilitate students' learning. The issue is

> ... *not simply to work harder at teaching but to work smarter—to engage students in more intensive and effective learning communities; to shift from passive to active approaches to learning; to shift from instructing students about things (covering subjects) to helping students learn how to do things (acquire complex abilities) and to acquire the deeper levels of knowledge we call understanding and judgment* (Edgerton 1993c, p. 6).

This restructuring of faculty roles will likely occur along the lines outlined earlier (see Guskin 1994). With the advent of the new technologies and the information available over the Internet, faculty will not—and could not—know all the information about a field. Besides, students will need to develop learning and information-processing skills to take advantage of the Internet and succeed in the future. Hypertext and CD-ROM technologies will encourage students to pursue self-paced and self-directed learning that will require faculty to perform less like "the sage on a stage" and more like "the guide on the side." If lecturing is too passive for students, faculty may opt to use simple technologies such as videotaped lessons or more advanced technologies to convey information to students, thereby freeing faculty time to interact with students at higher levels. Faculty will need to design, modify, and assess students' learning experiences and mentor students in their efforts to develop their abilities to the highest extent possible.

Some writers (e.g., Atkinson and Tuzin 1992) have maintained that focusing on students' learning will mean that faculty need to take greater personal responsibility for lower-division and general education courses. Currently, this level of instruction is delegated to graduate assistants, lecturers, and untenured professors. Although they may do an able job, their temporary or junior status belies a hidden message about the importance placed on their work.

A recent redefinition of educational quality deemphasizes inputs and traditional teaching and learning processes. It proposes instead that quality be driven by "fitness-for-use" criteria, whereby the goals of students' learning provide the "why" of education within which its curricula, processes, and teaching and learning methods are organized (Massy and Wilger 1996). Faculty manage the educational process, assess the process and students' achievement, and work to continuously improve it.

This transformation has been described as the building of a "national learning infrastructure" (Heterick 1995). Whereas the nation has an extraordinary *research* infrastructure comprising research universities and government laboratories and a *teaching* infrastructure comprising institutions of higher education that support the work of faculty, we lack a national *learning* infrastructure. Such an infrastructure would address higher education's need to improve quality, lower costs, increase access, and increase productivity.

Define Outputs

The push for greater accountability and for studies and reporting of faculty workload may be traced to a number of factors, not least of which may be the "inadequate ways of accounting for what students have learned" (Plater 1995, p. 25). With no way to measure or assess what students learn, external bodies have focused on the information that was available: measures of input (such as faculty workload or time spent in the classroom).

Thus, it is important that higher education undertake to define its product: what skills, knowledge, and competencies—and level of proficiency for each—we expect our graduates to possess. More simply, what does a baccalaureate degree mean in terms of these qualities? Is it a certain number of credit hours, a certain configuration of courses, or a "specified standard of competency at a certified level of quality"? (Plater 1995, p. 28). "We are no better than the students we graduate" (p. 29), and institutions can and will continue to be evaluated by the skills and experiences of its graduates. In fact, a time could come when students' learning outcomes are the only measure of an institution's productivity, and faculty workload will no longer be an issue of concern as long as the institution is producing evidence that students are learning and learning productively and well.

While Pascarella and Terenzini (1991) have done yeoman's work in compiling the extant research on the outcomes of

Thus, it is important that higher education undertake to define its product: what skills, knowledge, and competencies— and level of proficiency for each— we expect our graduates to possess.

college, their work is not well known outside academe. And while their work surveys the outcomes of college that have been researched and found to be consistent or significant across time or studies, it does not answer the question of what skills an institution intends its graduates to possess or what skills society needs those graduates to possess.

The outcomes of all types of faculty effort need to be more clearly defined before external intrusions cease. Faculty are an "asset," not only for the institution, but also for the public good (Layzell, Lovell, and Gill 1996). When viewed as a "state asset," the outcomes of faculty activity could be defined as (1) college graduates who can get jobs and advance in their careers, (2) a college education comparable to tuition charged, and (3) solutions to state social and economic concerns. Once outcomes are defined, institutions would be held accountable for producing the stated outcomes and left to do the job without further external oversight, other than an assessment of whether the outcomes are achieved and the negotiation of new outcomes. This model, however, depends upon higher education's ability to define its outputs and to reach agreement with its sponsors that these outputs are indeed the ones they desire and will support. It will undoubtedly be a difficult endeavor, but it is one that could reap important benefits in terms of public trust and support.

This discussion cannot be complete without returning to the issue of performance- and outcome-based funding models (Anderes 1995). As mentioned earlier, 15 states have versions of performance-based funding, with the usual approach being the allocation of a small percentage of the total appropriation depending on achievement of prescribed performance outcomes (see Ashworth 1994 for a review of the problems identified by Texas during planning for implementation of a proposed performance-based funding system). Despite the conceptual and practical problems, however, several states are considering making continued funding of higher education contingent on the delivery of the outcomes they value. Interest in performance-based funding is not likely to recede and may in fact grow as attempts to elucidate the outcomes produced by an institution's entire budget gain in popularity.

Clarify Curricula and Mission
Institutions and faculty need to determine the "essential knowledge in a discipline, as opposed to specialized research

or political interests" (Zemsky, Massy, and Oedel 1993, p. 58). This task is difficult and contentious, and will not be accomplished swiftly. Once focused, however, the curriculum will require "fewer courses, less specialization, more consolidation, . . . [and] smaller, less costly faculties" (p. 58).

Moreover, faculties need to focus attention on how current academic policies can encourage students to graduate with the basic education most employers expect. An analysis of college transcripts prepared by the U.S. Department of Education in 1992 (see Wingspread 1993) found that 26.2 percent of recent bachelor's degree recipients did not take a single credit in history, 30.8 percent did not study mathematics, 39.6 percent took no courses in English or American literature, and 58.4 percent graduated without a foreign language. Core curricula—or general education—need to be assured with the granting of the diploma.

Institutions should embrace different missions rather than continue to try to be all things to all people (Commission on National Investment 1997). Activities that are marginal to the mission should be eliminated and duplicative courses or programs pruned.

Perhaps the more important result of mission confusion has been the mismatch between the current missions of higher education institutions and the public's perception of what they should be doing (and what legislatures are willing to support). Remedying this mismatch will not be satisfied by a public relations campaign to convince the public that the current mission is the one taxpayers should be willing to support. It simply will not work.

What is needed are serious discussions among an institution's internal members—the faculty, administrators, students, and staff—and external constituents—legislators, business leaders, state representatives, and community members. Bringing customers—and bill payers—into the conversation will ensure that institutions modify self-interested behaviors with a realization that external constituencies are demanding to be served, served well, and at a justifiable cost.

To be helpful, however, this conversation will need to answer questions about fundamental purpose, including what should be delivered and to whom, as well as institutions' contributions to stability, change, economic benefits, and social issues (see Pew 1991). The answers will lead to a better allocation of scarce resources among the institution's prime responsibilities and the faculty's primary duties to teaching, research, and service. We can "stop pretending that everything [faculty] choose to do in their working lives is equally worthwhile, urgent, and deserving of institutional support" (Lovett 1995, p. B1). Instead, faculty would direct their efforts "toward teaching, research, and public service in a balance that meets state needs, not simply institutional aspirations" (Jordan and Layzell 1992, p. 13) or even personal priorities.

Realize the Potential of Technology
Technology has been characterized as a "transforming factor" and "paradigm shift in the offing" (Plater 1995, p. 24), a "powerful tool that can be dynamically and creatively applied" to academic restructuring (Stanford Forum 1995), because:

1. Technology provides students with the latitude to determine the ways they will learn, just as it certainly expands the amount of what can be learned.
2. It allows learning to occur at the time, place, and pace chosen by the student rather than the institution.
3. It enhances (rather than detracts from) the level of interaction possible between faculty and students, or among students, or with other experts at a distance from students.
4. It expands the amount of information available to students beyond the holdings of the local library and the knowledge of professors.
5. It makes available to students possibilities for learning offered by other higher education institutions or other providers.
6. It will enable higher education to provide services to students, where they are and when they need them, thereby placing the student in the center of the higher education enterprise.
7. It can help revise or replace administrative processes that will in turn conserve scarce resources and improve services.
8. It focuses faculty attention on learning outcomes for students and on the pedagogy to achieve them in a way that no previous teaching technology has accomplished.

Quite simply, technology will "change forever the dominant model of synchronous, time-linked interaction that has made teaching and learning complementary and interdependent" (Plater 1995, p. 25). Moreover, it will drive change throughout the organization as new ways of doing old activities are adopted and old assumptions are examined. These are heady changes. What will they mean for faculty work?

First, it may mean that faculty will not teach more, but less, in the traditional manner, and that they will teach differently (Mingle 1992). Second, it will enable the restructuring of faculty work from lecturer to facilitator of students' learning (as described by Guskin 1994), and it will facilitate encouraging students to take greater responsibility for their learning (see Johnstone 1993, 1996; see also Norris and MacDonald 1993). Third, it can be used to implement the "Seven Principles of Good Practice" (Chickering and Ehrmann 1996): encouraging contact between faculty and students, developing teamwork among students, using active learning techniques, providing prompt feedback, allowing increased time on task, conveying high expectations, and allowing different ways of learning. Although technology may not be sufficient to ensure students' learning, it is an important tool for encouraging the types of learning experiences that are conducive to students' learning.

The challenge to faculty will be to understand where technology can be an aid and where other methods would work better. Research is needed that helps faculty make wise decisions about the use of technology—research on what skills can be taught via technology (and which not), which disciplines might be more amenable to different technologies (and which not), which skills and knowledges can be learned via technology (and which not), and which students might learn more in this fashion (and which not). In fact, we need answers to many questions, and a nationwide effort seems in order so that quality research can guide us to best uses of technology.

The good news is that faculty are already adopting the new technologies: From 1989 to 1995, the percent of faculty using computers in all or most of their courses increased 6 percentage points, from 13 percent to 19 percent. Conversely, the percent of faculty using extensive lecturing in their courses declined 7 percentage points over the same time period, from 56 percent to 49 percent (Magner 1996a). (Lecturing, however, is still the predominant instructional mode, despite these changes.) Use of the Web and e-mail has been incorporated into 9 percent and 25 percent of college courses, respectively (Green 1997).

The challenge to faculty will be to understand where technology can be an aid and where other methods would work better.

All of these factors will allow technology to help higher education increase its productivity (see Green and Gilbert 1995; Heterick 1994; Massy and Zemsky 1995), which will occur by three means. First, technology may replace some of the faculty's activities, such as teaching through the traditional lecture, thereby freeing faculty time for activities that contribute to higher-level skills in students or make better use of the faculty's expertise (e.g., designing new courseware, pedagogical research, and assessment of students). Second, as students learn at the time, place, and pace of their own choosing, productive learning and progress to the proficiency levels outlined in our definition of the baccalaureate degree could increase. Further, technology will allow the customization of higher education, improving its value to students and the society being served. Third, technology can ease the "limits of time and space" for the institution as well, improving the productivity of its investment in faculty, staff, and physical space and helping to slow the rise in costs related to adding new faculty and staff, library holdings, and buildings.

Of course, some doubt that technology can significantly replace faculty—thereby replacing an investment in labor with an investment in capital—or that technology can "disintermediate" the teaching-learning enterprise so as to lessen the need for faculty and lower the number of faculty needed (Oberlin 1996). If this statement is true, then institutions cannot look to information technology as a way to decrease the personnel budget. But if it is true, technology shows evidence of contributing to increases in productivity through increased learning for students and perhaps faster movement of students through their studies.

Although the initial investment and continuing upkeep of the hardware and software will be substantial, whether or not the investment pays off will depend on how it is used. If technology is continually conceptualized as an "add-on," it will not result in the improved productivity it has the potential to produce. If, on the other hand, technology is applied in ways that help the institution restructure its core processes (e.g., teaching, student services) and replace capital for labor, gains in productivity can be realized in time (McGuinness and Ewell 1994; Massy and Zemsky 1995).

There is no doubt that building the technological infrastructure that an institution needs to support the new learning paradigm is a significant challenge in terms of adequate resources and expertise, especially for smaller institutions. While it is unfortunate that the need to invest in new technology arrives at the same time that states suffer from a number of demands for available resources, many states have invested heavily in these new tools and state networks, usually through one-time appropriations. Funding the ongoing costs of operations and upgrading seems to require the development of strategic investment plans on the part of the institution; in fall 1996, only 28 percent had such plans (Green 1997). This discussion would not be complete without also emphasizing the increased costs of personal computers, e-mail accounts, and access to the Web for students, who understand that they are necessary academic tools. Not surprisingly, students are increasingly willing to pay special technology fees to fund these resources, and 32 percent of campuses now require such a fee (Green 1997).

Admittedly, the route from today to the technologically assisted institution of the future will not be easy, and we will need to find appropriate ways to provide faculty with the technical and instructional support to help them learn and make the best use of the new technologies. However difficult this transformation may be, it is upon us and cannot be ignored.

Understand the Market
Perhaps one of the more important reasons that technology cannot be ignored is that it is also enabling an unprecedented growth in education—and noneducation—providers and services. It "is not well understood that the information highway makes possible a fundamental shift in the set of educational providers" (Zemsky 1996, p. 87). But the cable and telecommunications industries (and some new entrepreneurs) understand it, and they are combining forces to tap the educational market made possible by the explosion of the Internet into the home and the workplace.

Witness the explosion of the personal computer. In 1993, data from the census indicated that 45.8 percent of those surveyed used computers at work, 27.1 percent had a computer at home, and 59 percent of the students in the families surveyed used computers at school. And these figures have likely increased sharply since then. What is also interesting in this phenomenon is the large use of home computers for educational programs, or 34.6 percent of home use. This statistic is mirrored by growth in educational software. In 1990, prepackaged software generated $16.5 billion in sales; by 1994, sales had nearly doubled, to $27.7 billion.

Further, the increase in use of the Internet in the K–12 system will mean a change in the skills and experience of students entering higher education. In fall 1996, 65 percent of all public schools in the United States had access to the Internet, a gain of 15 percent in each of the previous two years (U.S. Dept. of Education 1997). The Internet's penetration into public elementary schools is 61 percent, 77 percent for public secondary schools. Thus, use of the Internet is happening during earlier grades, and it is becoming ever more likely that high school graduates will be familiar with its use. The student market is being altered—in terms of high school graduates' skills and expectations and perhaps as well in their willingness to enroll in higher education courses offered through alternative modes of delivery or through nontraditional providers.

The perception that accreditation will protect higher education from competition is also being abandoned as accrediting bodies fall into disrepute and struggle to redefine their legitimate purpose (Zemsky 1996). Business is increasing its criticisms of higher education, and the story about the high school graduate employed by Microsoft is told and retold with enthusiasm (a true story, by the way). So what prevents other providers from offering college degrees—and having their degrees accepted by employers?

"Delivery of high-bandwidth learning tools to the desktops of employees in leading-edge organizations" is under way (Norris 1996a, p. 3). In time, these same tools (and others) will be "available to every desktop, home entertainment center, school, business, and community learning center" (p. 3). It will be formidable competition to higher education, one that will not easily be met unless we understand this emerging marketplace much better.

To be successful in this new environment, institutions will need to provide competitive services and

> . . . demonstrate anew that they are best qualified to define the substance, standards, and processes of higher education. Failing that demonstration, traditionally cast colleges and universities will lose much of their power to define the public good in their own terms and hence their virtual monopoly over the credentialing function that higher education now fulfills (Pew 1996a, p. 3).

Another aspect of understanding the changed marketplace for postsecondary education, however, will be appreciating what students and their parents want from college. What they want certainly includes better and more appropriate preparation for the workplace as well as for citizenship, but at a cost that is affordable and reasonable in terms of the increased earnings derived from a college education. Increasingly, the competitiveness of the job market may mean that graduates with general skills cannot find employment easily, or at the level desired, while those with technical skills find high-wage jobs. Getting a good job that is secure and pays well is the goal of many who support education, despite the academy's often condescending view of vocationalism.

Although in the past we may have thought that what happens to graduates was not our concern, the public's view of colleges will be affected by our graduates' experiences in the marketplace. Thus, we would be wise to attend to ensuring their ultimate success, however vocational it may be.

The reward structure, which has effectively molded faculty behavior to follow the rewards of research, will require revision.

Realign Rewards for Research and Teaching

The reward structure, which has effectively molded faculty behavior to follow the rewards of research, will require revision. The good news is that many faculty already value their teaching role, and some efforts to improve the rewards for teaching are paying off in changing faculty priorities (Lunde and Barrett 1994). Others express more caution, noting it is "harder than you think" to promote excellent teaching (Gibbs 1995). It will require higher education to define, weight, and promote excellent teaching and to provide training for faculty who may need to first learn competent, then excellent, teaching skills. Changing the faculty reward structure will require substantial administrative support and leadership, as well as faculty involvement, as rewards are realigned to more nearly reflect the emerging institutional mission (Diamond 1993).

While much has been made of the academy's overemphasis on research, it is clear that society continues to need high-quality, relevant research, whether basic or applied. Several questions may need to be addressed: how research is defined, its relative importance, who does it, how it is funded, and its appropriate reward.

The effort to redefine scholarly pursuits to incorporate a broader definition of appropriate intellectual and creative enterprise (Boyer 1990) has begun to bear fruit. By including the scholarship of integration, pedagogy, and application in addition to the predominant model of the scholarship of discovery, it is more likely that the scholarly activities of faculty can be more easily justified and explained to the funding public. A fifth scholarship—of engagement—has been proposed (Metzler 1994), wherein faculty actively use their considerable knowledge and expertise to assume a role as leaders for effecting change in society. Perhaps the new "scholarships" will contribute to improvements within the academy and in the surrounding community that those who currently question the relevance of much of today's research can clearly appreciate.

Fortunately, as many as 20 professional associations are working on broadening the definition of professionally appropriate research (Diamond 1994), and this effort will go a long way toward helping institutions realign research with institutional and community needs. With a more flexible definition of research acceptable to the discipline, faculty careers would less likely suffer a penalty.

These efforts show promise. The effort to "allow and reward the serious pursuit of the big picture" should be stressed rather than continued pursuit of research that is overly specialized, disconnected, and esoteric (Marien 1996). Society needs integrated information to offset the growing "infoglut." Other efforts must look at how to shift the emphasis from quantity of research to its quality (see Scott and Awbrey 1993 for a model for transforming scholarship with the ultimate end of creating a better and wiser world). Traditional scholarship was linear, rational, and separate. It was linear in the sense that theory was developed first, then applied. It was rational, dealing only with facts and excluding values and emotions. It was separate, with each discipline pursuing its own lines of inquiry without impacting or learning from other types of scholarship. The goal will be to make the new scholarship fully integrated across multiple ways of knowing and multiple lines of inquiry.

Because faculty rewards currently stress the importance of research (see Diamond and Adam 1993; Fairweather 1992), redressing the imbalance between teaching and research will require aligning rewards with the institution's mission (Heydinger and Simsek 1992; Mingle 1992). We must find ways to tie salary and other nonfinancial rewards to an institutional mission that stresses high-quality teaching *and* research.

It is not clear whether investigating the effect research and instruction have on each other—whether they support or compete with each other—has any benefit. Whether good teachers can do research or good researchers can be excellent teachers is an interesting question, but answers may rely on personal characteristics more than we would like to admit. Some people do both well, and others do one better than the other. And there may be nothing in the nature of either teaching or research that precludes excellence in both activities except the ability of the particular practitioner.

While research will continue to play an "important role in research and public policy formulation," it will not involve "all faculty at all times" (Plater 1995, p. 31). A single model for all faculty conducting research throughout their careers may no longer be tenable. Further, research will likely become "more applied and focused" and "tied to the mission of the institution instead of the discretion of the individual faculty" (p. 31). Some analysts maintain that research will likely become the province of the research institutions and be increasingly less the province of other types of institutions.

Other writers focus on ways to make research a better investment. One suggestion is that research funded by institutions—much of it from state dollars if the institution is publicly funded—be made more like research funded by granting agencies or publishers (Miles 1994). Instead of supporting research activities "automatically," institutions would fund research on the basis of the project, with a set schedule for completion and expectation of a research product. Faculty without a funded research project would fill their schedules with teaching.

A final word should be said about the role of academic freedom in an institution whose rewards have been realigned to more nearly match institutional and societal priorities. Academic freedom of speech and economic security should be preserved, but the faculty's independence, without direction or orientation to others' priorities, must be changed (Plater 1995). "Academic freedom means a great deal, but it should not mean freedom from responsibility to students" (Kennedy 1995, p. 12). Thus, the purpose, rights, and responsibilities of tenure and academic freedom in the new higher education may need to be revised (see Magrath 1997; Rice 1996). This revision will most likely involve retaining important qualities from the past but also recasting the faculty's responsibilities to better support the necessary work of the future. Some evidence suggests that many faculty recognize the need to revise some traditional practices to be more in line with the needs of modern universities. A recent publication by faculty at the State University of New York and California State University (1997) recognizes that tenure should not be a barrier to academic productivity or responsible management.

In other words, the reward structure needs to encourage the realignment of faculty commitments in support of the institution's mission, which has in time also been realigned to better support its role in society. On a higher level, faculty have been called on to "revitalize the social contract that binds faculty to one another, to students, and to the institution to which they owe primary allegiance" (Pew 1992b, p. 2A). Evidence suggests that many faculty are willing to engage in this effort.

Make Costs Clear

How can costs be controlled or productivity improved if the cost of certain actions or assumptions are not made clear and real to the people making the decisions? If costs are the problem of "someone else," then people are left in ignorance to continue contributing to the problem. Conversely, to elicit the understanding and cooperation of everyone in the institution, it is important that the cost implications of decisions be made more explicit.

Budgeting should be decentralized to the operational unit—the academic department—so that departmental members can face the "consequences of their decisions" (Levin 1993, p. 4; see also Massy and Zemsky 1991). One possible approach is to ensure that units receive credit for income generated but are also charged for all of their expenses (Levin 1993). The decentralization of resources would mean that "faculty [have] a stake in the positive consequences of reallocation" (Massy and Zemsky 1991, p. 7). Such an approach could encourage improvement in performance-based assessment and internal accountability for financial management (Commission on National Investment 1997).

Fortunately, a number of writers are attempting to understand the costs of higher education so that institutions can be more productive. The results of a symposium on productivity in higher education (Anderson and Meyerson 1992) and the work of Massy and Zemsky provide ways to make the cost implications of decisions and structures clear to participants. In fact, a number of cost-benefit analyses on distance education and technology-enhanced education are under way. It is likely that these efforts will result in a growing number of guides for improving productivity.

Think Creatively, Restructure Seriously, Experiment Vigorously

The challenges facing higher education require the minds, hearts, and emotions of our institutions' members—faculty, staff, administrators, and students. We have substantial and long-standing assumptions to rethink, processes to revise, and behaviors to relearn. And we cannot do these things without the creativity, seriousness, and willingness of individuals to experiment in order to develop potential solutions and then to test, evaluate, and modify them.

The necessary restructuring is threefold (Eaton 1995). Restructuring higher education *resources* will require rethinking revenue flows and the sources of funding. Restructuring *uses* of those revenues will require more than simple budget cutting; it will also require revising instructional processes to be more productive and improving the institution's accountability for its use of resources. And restructuring *results* will require deliberately changing expectations for what higher education does and delivers to the society that supports it. All three types of restructuring will likely be needed to ensure the future health of the higher education enterprise.

The crisis faced by higher education is one of imagination (Myers 1993). And imagination—the ability to not "take too many things for granted," to ask the right questions, and to "bring some of our sacred cows in from the pasture" (p. 5)— is what is needed. Business calls it "thinking outside the box."

Dealing with the problems will require seriously considering the viewpoints of outsiders rather than indulging in denial or wishful thinking that these problems will fade away or the critics will tire and expend their energy on some other hapless public servant. Restructuring will require a spirit of experimentation, for the restructured institution of 2001 cannot be described. We will need a willingness to try untested ideas and suspend our need to know all of the possible outcomes before taking the first step, to overanalyze as a defense against making changes (Guskin 1996).

Higher education has these qualities in abundance: Its artists are creative, its professionals serious about their work, and its scientists experimenters of the highest order. The difference, of course, is a basic one; the objects of our creativity, our seriousness, and our experimentation will be ourselves and our institutions.

The question remains whether change will be incremental or cataclysmic. Some believe that "incremental change will not work, not this time" (Plater 1995, p. 33). Institutions should not "just tinker at the margins; it will only ensure that higher education limps through the decade" (Stine, cited in Pew 1991, p. 5A).

Because incremental change does not noticeably affect the basic underlying processes of an institution or the underlying belief systems, it is often accepted after some discussion; it is also easy to conceive of because it is consistent with how people have practiced their professions. But incremental changes do not deal with the type of structural changes necessary for a future of reduced resources, increased availability of and demand for powerful technologies, and the demand that a college or university be accountable for student learning outcomes (Guskin 1996, p. 32).

If this assessment of the situation is accurate, incremental change will be a tool to arrive at more substantial changes but cannot be the only satisfactory response. Thus, helping faculty and staff deal with changes that will inevitably involve major alterations in the assumptions, values, and character of their work will be necessary.

Hold the Entire Community Responsible
The monograph "Shared Purposes" outlines the forces that have kept administrators and faculty at cross-purposes and the reasons that they must "build together an environment of trust and support" (Pew 1996b, p. 10). No one group of individuals can set themselves apart from the problems facing higher education, concerned only for their own part of the enterprise, for "ownership of a part implies responsibility for the integrity of the whole" (p. 10).

Moreover, "no single leader or single constituent group can make much progress alone; . . . faculty, administrators, governing boards, state officials—stakeholders everywhere must, for a change, work *together* for constructive reform" (Edgerton 1993c, p. 5). This situation argues for a democratic approach to developing new ideas and new approaches, encouraging both junior staff and senior members of the institution to make contributions.

Faculty face two challenges. First, they must accept ownership for the health of their institutions and the communities where they reside. They need to take an active role in developing approaches and a cooperative attitude to problem solving. Second, the community of faculty must also work together to solve increasingly multidimensional problems through a multidisciplinary approach. Greater collaboration (Rice 1996) and teamwork (Plater 1995) must be pursued to maximize the expertise of individuals and help address issues of workload and productivity.

The community within higher education and those outside who care about its future must find ways to ensure that individuals see their institutions' viability as their responsibility. Leadership alone cannot mandate outcomes; organizations are far too interdependent to have change dictated from the top. Thus, it is the individual who decides to change who, in the final analysis, holds the future of the organization in his or her hands.

Encourage New Leaders and Fresh Ideas

Stressing the need for the community to take responsibility for solving the problems besetting higher education should not preclude the need for new leaders and ideas. Neither should the need for leaders preclude the development of a strong community. We need both.

Leaders come from several places in an organization. It was Vice Chancellor Robert Diamond at Syracuse University, for example, who first surveyed faculty and administrators about the balance between teaching and research (Edgerton 1993b). In 1990, Stanford University President Donald Kennedy called teaching "the first among our labors" and followed with ideas for changing the faculty reward system. Later in 1990, University of California President David Gardner created a task force on faculty rewards that called for broader forms of scholarship and peer review of teaching. Leadership at the University of Michigan challenged the traditional belief that controlling costs would necessarily harm quality and proclaimed that "cost containment (and even cost reduction) can go hand in hand with quality improvement" (Zemsky and Massy 1990, p. 16).

But leadership need not always come from the presidential suite, for often "the bottleneck is at the top of the bottle"

(Norris 1996b, p. 7). Our pyramidal organizations—with actual leadership or the only perceived leadership coming from the top—can be counterproductive to change. To unstop the bottleneck, it may be necessary to manage leaders who do not lead (Guskin 1996). Those who are committed to change must first build support among key faculty and administrators, who would then provide the president or provost with the "means and opportunity to lead" through collaboration with dedicated leaders throughout the organization (Guskin 1996).

Thus, new ideas and leaders may well come from individuals throughout the enterprise: from junior faculty and new staff members, from senior faculty and experienced administrators.

Thus, new ideas and leaders may well come from individuals throughout the enterprise: from junior faculty and new staff members, from senior faculty and experienced administrators. This "subversive" strategy (Norris 1996b), with its ability to question assumptions, fortunately can come from anywhere in the organization. Moreover, everyone can be the leader at some time, and even the oddest of new ideas can have the nugget of a great idea within it.

Higher education especially may need "visionary leadership" at the current time (Wilson 1996). Higher education needs leaders who can provide a vision of what higher education can and should be. But only when that vision is shared and a commitment exists to act on the vision will the vision be a guiding force for the everyday actions of members of the organization. Vision is a "field," a "thinking into the future, creating a destination for the organization" (Wheatley 1992, p. 53). But "field creation is not just a task for senior managers. Every employee has energy to contribute [to the field]" (p. 56), and a clear vision and set of organizational values must be disseminated to "all corners of the organization, involve everyone, and be available everywhere" (p. 55). Doing so allows everyone to act on the vision and make appropriate contributions to furthering the organization's goals.

Embrace the Dichotomies

It may not seem fair to have a future that is unclear and a present that is shaky at best. Moreover, this review of the literature has uncovered a number of themes for the future that are contradictory yet must be pursued at the same time. Although it may sound confusing, it is not.

Several conflicting directives have been urged on universities. They should:

• Be more business-like (that is, focus on the bottom line)

and less business-like (focus on maintaining ideals and not merely on the bottom line);

- Do more scientific research (to help with economic competitiveness) *and* less research (and focus more on teaching and public service);
- Increase the quality and quantity of services *and* cut costs; and
- Be both the guardians *and* the critics of our cultural inheritance (President's Council 1992, p. 21).

If these ends seem impossible to achieve, that nevertheless makes them no less essential to the future of higher education.

The future has been cast into similar contrary trends, with forces that drive higher education toward both standardization *and* individualization and toward both centralization *and* decentralization (Plater 1995, p. 27). While one would be understandably sympathetic of anyone facing mutually exclusive forces, sympathy may not be sufficient to survive the countervailing forces facing higher education today. What may be required is the ability to distinguish when standardization is required and when individualization is the better choice, which processes are best centralized and which could be decentralized (at least temporarily).

Institutions will likely need to become more separate—more individualized in their missions—and also more interdependent (Pew 1995). In other words, institutions will need to craft specific, well-honed missions that address the needs of special markets as well as look for appropriate ways to collaborate with other institutions to ensure that students move easily between institutions, new opportunities are pursued, and resources are shared.

To some, contradictions are especially fruitful. Conflicts and contradictions "create order" by stirring things up and roiling the pot, "looking always for those disturbances that challenge and disrupt until, finally, things become so jumbled that we reorganize work at a new level of efficiency" (Wheatley 1992, p. 166).

This upcoming period will be interesting, to say the least.

Serve Others
Perhaps we do not need to look too far for a vision with the power to gain consensus and commitment to action. It can be found in the past, and in our current values.

With establishment of the land-grant colleges, higher education became an "instrument of direct service to the nation" (Rice 1996, p. 4). In 1908, Harvard's President Eliot claimed that "American institutions of higher education are filled with the modern democratic spirit of serviceableness. Teachers and students alike are profoundly moved by the desire to serve the democratic community" (p. 5). If higher education's past stressed service and this value is still active in its psyche, we can restructure institutions with an eye toward making them better servants of society.

Service is important to the community at large (Plater 1995). Colleges will "not only have an obligation to apply their knowledge and expertise in the solution of problems, but they have to do so in a timely fashion with immediate and demonstrable results" (p. 32). The institution is a servant, and it should feel itself neither demeaned nor of lesser value for finding a practical use for its theoretical knowledge.

A system can change in an "autopoetic" fashion, changing in a way that remains consistent with itself or its prior manifestations (Wheatley 1992). Organizations must be open to environmental information that may even contradict current understandings rather than protect themselves from external forces and unwanted conflict. Higher education institutions, confronted with the need to change, will be able to make appropriate adjustments by maintaining the best of their past values, such as service to others.

Conclusions

The good news—and there is a great deal of it to be found in a review of the literature calling attention to higher education's ills—is that colleges and universities are blessed and burdened by an overabundance of "smarts" (Zemsky 1996, p. 82). Faculty are "too smart to miss what's going on" (p. 84), and we must depend on the application of those smarts to find solutions to problems and to design the higher education institution of the future. Fortunately, some evidence suggests that faculty groups are recognizing these issues (State University 1997) and are committed to helping institutions resolve problems in a way that helps students and retains important core values of higher education.

The issue about faculty workload is not to ask faculty to work longer hours, but to ask them to work smarter and to more closely align their efforts with the requirements for students' learning, institutional priorities, and society's needs. States need to rely on their higher education institutions to help address the problems they face: providing increased access, controlling rising costs, and improving productivity. Thus, when higher education institutions become part of the solution rather than contributors to the problem, states may view them differently, initiating an era of trust and mutual respect. Though trust must be earned, higher education certainly possesses the native "smarts" to earn it many times over.

APPENDIX: Annotated Bibliography of Faculty Workload Studies

Arizona. The Joint Legislative Budget Committee (Arizona Joint 1992) surveyed full-time faculty about average hours spent per week on several activities. Total average workload was 56.3 hours, with 8.9 hours spent in direct classroom instruction, 14 hours in preparation for class, and 3.5 hours in individualized instruction (see also Jordan and Layzell 1992).

California. A survey conducted in 1990 of a sample of permanent faculty at California State University and faculty at four comparable institutions tested the hypothesis that no differences existed in average workload. The survey compared faculty workload by institutional size, academic rank, discipline, and demographic characteristics of faculty.

Colorado. The Colorado Commission on Higher Education (1994) reported average faculty teaching workload (as defined by sections taught) for faculty types (tenure/nontenure track, teaching assistants, others). It also reported on measures of faculty productivity (e.g., student credit hours generated per FTE faculty, average sections taught).

Idaho. The Idaho Board of Education (1993) used existing data to report on total faculty workload, workload by activity (teaching, research, and service), contact hours, and other teaching activities, student credit hours generated by faculty rank, and distribution of student enrollments across class sizes.

Illinois. The Illinois Board of Higher Education (1993) initiated a statewide system and institution-level discussion of faculty roles and responsibilities across instruction, research, and public service, including discussions of faculty development and productivity, as part of its PQP (Priorities*Quality*Productivity) initiative.

Minnesota. The Minnesota Higher Education Coordinating Board (1993) collected data on workload for full-time faculty in response to a legislative directive. It found variations in data that limited comparisons. Differences in faculty workload were correlated to institutional mission.

Montana. The Montana Office of the Legislative Auditor (1990) collected data from select academic departments (e.g., business, education, English, mathematics) on average weekly hours and hours spent by category (instruction, research, service).

Nebraska. The Nebraska Legislative Fiscal Office (1992) collected data from full-time faculty during fall 1991 to answer specific legislative questions relating to the balance among instruction, research, and service; average credit hours taught; total credit hours generated; use of full- and part-time faculty and teaching assistants; and section sizes. Data varied by academic department, institutional mission, and departmental function (general education, major, graduate).

New York. The New York Office of the State Comptroller (1990) found variations in student/faculty ratios and a number of low-enrollment courses at the State University of New York. The study did not report noninstructional activities.

Ohio. Faculty and institutional representatives (Ohio Study Committee 1992) prepared information on workload for full-time faculty, which documented that 56.3 percent of time was spent on instruction and that workload varied by institutional mission, and provided workload data in ranges. The Ohio Board of Regents (1994) prepared standards and guidelines for workload.

Oregon. The Oregon State System of Higher Education (1997) provided an overview of faculty work, productivity, and workload, and a profile of the faculty.

South Dakota. The South Dakota Board of Regents (1994) used existing databases to provide estimates of percent of effort for teaching, research, and service. The information was used to assess the standard 12-hour teaching load, which may differ by department and can be offset by other assignments.

Texas. The Texas Higher Education Coordinating Board (1993) used an existing database to provide longitudinal data on a different measure of workload: semester credits hours (SCH) generated and average SCH over time for 1983 to 1992. Data documented an increase in faculty (with larger increases in teaching assistants and part-time faculty) and SCHs generated (except for tenured faculty), and a slight decline in average SCH for tenured faculty. A report on faculty workload by the Texas Office of the State Auditor (1994) documented the number of courses and credit hours by department at Texas research institutions.

Virginia. A survey by the State Council of Higher Education for Virginia (1991) reported that faculty worked 52 hours per week, spent 55 percent of their time on instruction-related activities, and preferred to work on research. Average weekly contact hours differed by institutional mission.

Washington. A survey of faculty by the Washington Higher Education Coordinating Board (1994) reported that faculty worked over 50 hours per week, with the majority of time devoted to instruction-related activities. Average weekly classroom contact hours differed by faculty rank, discipline, and mission.

Wisconsin. The Wisconsin Legislative Audit Bureau (1993) used existing data sources to provide longitudinal information on how faculty spent their time in the University of Wisconsin system. The study concluded that faculty spent less time with undergraduates, that teaching load had declined, and that teaching assistants taught 45.6 percent of lower-division courses at the research institutions.

REFERENCES

The Educational Resources Information Center (ERIC) Clearing-house on Higher Education abstracts and indexes the current litera-ture on higher education for inclusion in ERIC's database and an-nouncement in ERIC's monthly bibliographic journal, *Resources in Education* (RIE). Most of these publications are available through the ERIC Document Reproduction Service (EDRS). For publications cited in this bibliography that are available from EDRS, ordering number and price code are included. Readers who wish to order a publication should write to the ERIC Document Reproduction Ser-vice, 7420 Fullerton Road, Suite 110, Springfield, Virginia 22153-2852. (Phone orders with VISA or MasterCard are taken at 800/443-ERIC or 703/440-1400.) When ordering, please specify the docu-ment (ED) number. Documents are available as noted in microfiche (MF) and paper copy (PC). If you have the price code ready when you call, EDRS can quote an exact price. The last page of the latest issue of *Resources in Education* also has the current cost, listed by code.

American Association of University Professors. 1994. *The Work of Faculty: Expectations, Priorities, and Rewards*. Washington, D.C.: Author.

————. 1996. "Not So Bad." *Academe* 81: 14–93.

Anderes, Thomas. August 1995. "Outcome-Based Budgeting: Con-necting Budget Development, Allocation, and Outcomes." Paper presented to the State Higher Education Finance Officers. ED 394 402. 27 pp. MF–01; PC–02.

Anderson, Richard E., and Joel W. Meyerson. 1992. *Productivity and Higher Education: Improving the Effectiveness of Faculty, Facilities, and Financial Resources*. Princeton, N.J.: Peterson's Guides.

Arizona Joint Legislative Budget Committee. February 1992. "Faculty Teaching Loads at Arizona Universities." Phoenix: Author.

Ashworth, Kenneth H. November/December 1994. "Performance-Based Funding in Higher Education: The Texas Case Study." *Change* 26: 8–15.

Association of Higher Education Facilities Officers and National As-sociation of College and University Business Officers. 1996. *A Foundation to Uphold*. Alexandria, Va.: APPA Publications. ED 406 919. 199 pp. MF–01; PC not available EDRS.

Astin, Alexander W. 1993. *What Matters in College?* San Francisco: Jossey-Bass.

Astin, Alexander W., W.S. Korn, and Eric L. Dey. 1991. *The Ameri-can College Teacher: National Norms for the 1989–90 HERI*

Faculty Survey. Los Angeles: Higher Education Research Institute. ED 351 906. 163 pp. MF–01; PC not available EDRS.

Atkinson, Robert C., and Donald Tuzin. May/June 1992. "Equi-
librium in the Research University." *Change* 24: 20–31.

Bader, Jeanne. January/February 1995. "The Effects of 'Uncapping.'"
Academe 80: 36–37.

Barr, Robert B., and John Tagg. November/December 1995. "From
Teaching to Learning: A New Paradigm for Undergraduate Education." *Change* 27: 13–25.

Bentley, Richard, and Robert Blackburn. August 1990. "Changes in
Academic Research Performance over Time: A Study of Institutional Accumulative Advantage." *Research in Higher Education* 31: 327–53.

Blackburn, Robert T., and Richard J. Bentley. December 1993.
"Faculty Research Productivity: Some Moderators of Associated
Stressors." *Research in Higher Education* 34: 725–45.

Blackburn, Robert T., and Janet H. Lawrence. 1995. *Faculty at
Work.* Baltimore: Johns Hopkins Univ. Press.

Boggs, George R. December/January 1995–96. "The Learning Paradigm." *Community College Journal* 66: 24–27.

Bowen, Howard R. 1980. *The Costs of Higher Education: How Much
Do Colleges and Universities Spend per Student and How Much
Should They Spend?* San Francisco: Jossey-Bass.

Boyer, Ernest L. 1990. *Scholarship Reconsidered: Priorities of the
Professoriate.* Princeton, N.J.: Carnegie Foundation for the Advancement of Teaching. ED 326 149. 151 pp. MF–01; PC not
available EDRS.

Breneman, David W. February 1995. "A State of Emergency?" San
Jose: California Higher Education Policy Center. ED 380 002. 28
pp. MF–01; PC–02.

Breneman, David, and Joni Finney. April 1997. "The Changing
Landscape: Higher Education Finance in the 1990s." In *Shaping
the Future.* San Jose: California Higher Education Policy Center.

Brinkman, Paul T. 1992. "Factors That Influence Costs in Higher
Education." In *Containing Costs and Improving Productivity in
Higher Education,* edited by Carol S. Hollins. New Directions for
Institutional Research No. 75. San Francisco: Jossey-Bass.

Business Officer. May 1991. Monthly publication of National Association of College and University Business Officers (NACUBO).

California Higher Education Policy Center. 1996. *Shared Responsibility.* San Jose: Author.

———. Winter 1997. "New Survey Results." *Crosstalk* 5: 1+.

Callan, Patrick, and Joni E. Finney. June 1993. "By Design or De-

fault?" San Jose: California Higher Education Policy Center. ED
359 892. 17 pp. MF–01; PC–01.

Centra, John A. 1983. "Research Productivity and Teaching Effectiveness." *Research in Higher Education* 18: 379–89.

————. September/October 1994. "The Use of the Teaching
Portfolio and Student Evaluations for Summative Evaluation."
Journal of Higher Education 65: 555–70.

Chan, Susy S., and John Burton. April 1995. "Faculty Vitality in the
Comprehensive University: Changing Context and Concerns."
Research in Higher Education 36: 219–34.

Chickering, Arthur W., and Stephen C. Ehrmann. October 1996.
"Implementing the Seven Principles: Technology as Lever."
AAHE Bulletin 49: 3–6.

Clotfelter, Charles T. 1996. *Buying the Best: Cost Escalation in Elite
Higher Education.* Princeton, N.J.: Princeton Univ. Press.

Cochran, Leslie H. 1992. *Publish or Perish: The Wrong Issue.* Cape
Girardeau, Mo.: StepUp Inc.

College and University Personnel Association. 1996. *1995–96 Administrative Compensation Survey.* Washington, D.C.: Author.

Colorado Commission on Higher Education. November 1994.
"CCHE Faculty Productivity Data." Denver: Author.

Commission on National Investment in Higher Education. November
1997. "Breaking the Social Contract." *http://www.rand.org/publi-
cations/CAE/CAE100/.*

Cooper, Pamela A., and Oliver D. Hensley. 1993. "Faculty Perceptions of Measures of Activity and Productivity." Paper presented at a meeting of the Association for Institutional Research,
May 16–19, 1993, Chicago, Illinois. ED 360 911. 29 pp. MF–01;
PC–02.

Creswell, John W. 1985. *Faculty Research Performance: Lessons
from the Sciences and Social Sciences.* ASHE-ERIC Higher Education Report No. 4. Washington, D.C.: Association for the Study
of Higher Education. ED 267 677. 92 pp. MF–01; PC–04.

Daly, William T. January/February 1994. "Teaching and Scholarship:
Adapting American Higher Education to Hard Times." *Journal of
Higher Education* 65: 45–57.

Dey, Eric L. Spring 1994. "Dimensions of Faculty Stress: A Recent
Survey." *Review of Higher Education* 17: 305–22.

Diamond, Robert M. Spring 1993. "Instituting Change in the Faculty
Reward System." In *Recognizing Faculty Work: Reward Systems
for the Year 2000,* edited by Robert Diamond and Bronwyn
Adam. New Directions for Higher Education No. 81. San Francisco: Jossey-Bass.

————. 11 May 1994. "The Tough Task of Reforming the Faculty-Rewards System." *Chronicle of Higher Education:* B1–B3.

Diamond, Robert M., and Bronwyn E. Adam, eds. 1993. *Recognizing Faculty Work: Reward Systems for the Year 2000.* New Directions for Higher Education No. 81. San Francisco: Jossey-Bass.

Dillman, Donald A., James A. Christenson, Priscilla Salant, and Paul D. Warner. September 1995. *What the Public Wants from Higher Education: Workforce Implications from a 1995 National Survey.* Pullman, Wash.: Social and Economic Sciences Research Center. ED 388 193. 54 pp. MF–01; PC–03.

Dolence, Michael G., and Donald M. Norris. 1995. *Transforming Higher Education.* Ann Arbor, Mich.: Society for College and University Planning.

D'Souza, Dinesh. 1991. *Illiberal Education.* New York: Macmillan.

Dua, Jagdish. 1994. "Job Stressors and Their Effects on Physical Health, Emotional Health, and Job Satisfaction in a University." *Journal of Educational Administration* 32: 59–78.

Dunn, John A., Jr. 1992. "Retrench or Else: Public and Private Institutional Responses." In *Containing Costs and Improving Productivity in Higher Education,* edited by Carol S. Hollins. New Directions for Institutional Research No. 75. San Francisco: Jossey-Bass.

Eaton, Judith S. January 1995. "Investing in American Higher Education: An Argument for Restructuring." Paper presented to the Commission on National Investment in Higher Education. ED 378 906. 25 pp. MF–01; PC not available EDRS.

Edgerton, Russell. June 1993a. "The New Public Mood and What It Means for Higher Education." *AAHE Bulletin* 46: 3–7.

————. July/August 1993b. "The Reexamination of Faculty Priorities." *Change* 25: 10–25.

————. July/August 1993c. "The Tasks Faculty Perform." *Change* 25: 4–6.

El-Khawas, Elaine. 1992. *Campus Trends 1992.* Washington, D.C.: American Council on Education. ED 347 922. 93 pp. MF–01; PC–04.

————. 1995. *Campus Trends 1995.* Washington, D.C.: American Council on Education. ED 386 089. 67 pp. MF–01; PC–03.

Elman, Sandra E. Summer 1994. "Regional Accreditation and the Evaluation of Faculty." *Metropolitan Universities: An International Forum* 5: 71–78.

Elway Research, Inc. 1995. "Washington State Residents' Views of Higher Education." Seattle: Author.

Ewell, Peter T. November/December 1994a. "Accountability and the

Future of Self-Regulation." *Change* 26: 25–29.

———. Summer 1994b. "Restoring Our Links with Society: The Neglected Art of Collective Responsibility." *Metropolitan Universities* 5: 79–87.

Fairweather, James S. 1992. *Teaching and the Faculty Reward Structure: Relationships between Faculty Activities and Compensation.* University Park: Pennsylvania State Univ., National Center for Postsecondary Teaching, Learning, and Assessment. ED 357 699. 407 pp. MF–01; PC–17.

———. July/August 1993. "Faculty Rewards Reconsidered: The Nature of Trade-offs." *Change* 25: 44–47.

Feldman, Kenneth A. 1987. "Research Productivity and Scholarly Accomplishment of College Teachers as Related to Their Instructional Effectiveness." *Research in Higher Education* 26: 227–98.

Fellman, Gordon. January/February 1995. "On the Fetishism of Publications and the Secrets Thereof." *Academe* 81: 26–35.

Gibbs, Graham. May/June 1995. "Promoting Excellent Teaching Is Harder Than You'd Think." *Change* 27: 17–20.

Gmelch, Walter H., Nicholas P. Lovrich, and Phyllis Kay Wilke. 1984. "Sources of Stress in Academe: A National Perspective." *Research in Higher Education* 20: 477–90.

Gold, Steven D. 1995. *The Fiscal Crisis of the States.* Washington, D.C.: Georgetown Univ. Press.

Grassmuck, Karen. 28 March 1990. "Big Increases in Academic Support Staff Prompt Growing Concerns on Campuses." *Chronicle of Higher Education:* 32–33.

———. 14 August 1991. "Throughout the 80s, Colleges Hired More Nonteaching Staff Than Other Employees." *Chronicle of Higher Education:* 22.

Gray, Peter J., Robert C. Froh, and Robert M. Diamond. 1992. "A National Study of Research Universities: On the Balance between Research and Undergraduate Teaching." Syracuse, N.Y.: Syracuse Univ., Center for Instructional Development. ED 350 967. 23 pp. MF–01; PC–01.

Green, Kenneth C. 1997. "1996 Campus Computing Survey." ED 405 762. 38 pp. MF–01; PC not available EDRS. *http://ericir.syr. edu/Projects/Campus_computing.*

Green, Kenneth C., and Steven W. Gilbert. January/February 1995. "Academic Productivity and Technology." *Academe* 81: 19–25.

Guskin, Alan E. July/August 1994. "Restructuring the Role of Faculty." *Change* 26: 16–25.

———. September/October 1996. "Facing the Future: The Change

Process in Restructuring Universities." *Change* 28: 27–37.

Hampel, Robert L. April 1995. "Overextended." *Educational Researcher* 24: 29–30+.

Harvey, James, and Associates. 1994. *First Impressions and Second Thoughts: Public Support for Higher Education.* Washington, D.C.: American Council on Education.

Harvey, James, and John Immerwahr. 1995a. *The Fragile Coalition: Public Support for Higher Education in the 1990s.* Washington, D.C.: American Council on Education.

————. 1995b. *Goodwill and Growing Worry: Public Perceptions of American Higher Education.* Washington, D.C.: American Council on Education.

Hauke, Ray. August 1994. "An Update on Faculty Workload Activities among State Higher Education Systems." Paper presented to the State Higher Education Fiscal Officers.

Hekelman, Francine P., Stephen J. Zyzanski, and Susan A. Flocke. April 1995. "Successful and Less Successful Research Performance of Junior Faculty." *Research in Higher Education* 36: 235–55.

Heterick, Robert C., Jr. Spring 1994. "Technological Change and Higher Education Policy." *AGB Priorities* 1: 1–11.

————. 1995. "A National Learning Infrastructure." Paper presented to the Northwest Academic Forum, Portland, Oregon.

Heydinger, Richard B. October/November 1994. "A Reinvented Model for Higher Education." *On the Horizon* 3: 1–5.

Heydinger, Richard B., and Hasan Simsek. 1992. "An Agenda for Reshaping Faculty Productivity." Denver: State Higher Education Executive Officers. ED 356 727. 38 pp. MF–01; PC–02.

Hines, Edward R. 1996. *State Higher Education Appropriations, 1995–96.* Denver: State Higher Education Executive Officers. ED 399 855. 56 pp. MF–01; PC–03.

Hines, Edward R., and J. Russell Higham III. 1996. "Faculty Workload and State Policy." Paper presented at a meeting of the Association for the Study of Higher Education, November, Memphis, Tennessee.

Hodgkinson, Harold L. 1992. "A Demographic Look at Tomorrow." Washington, D.C.: Center for Demographic Policy. ED 359 087. 23 pp. MF–01; PC not available EDRS.

Huber, Robert M. 1992. *How Professors Play the Cat Guarding the Cream: Why We're Paying More and Getting Less in Higher Education.* Lanham, Md.: George Mason Univ. Press.

Idaho Board of Education. 1993. "Faculty Workload Study." Boise: Author.

Illinois Board of Higher Education. 1993. *Enhancing Quality and Productivity in Illinois Higher Education: Faculty Roles and Responsibilities.* Springfield: Author.

Immerwahr, John, and Jill Boese. March 1995. "Preserving the Higher Education Legacy." Sacramento: California Higher Education Policy Center. ED 381 069. 43 pp. MF–01; PC–02.

Immerwahr, John, and Steve Farkas. September 1993. "The Closing Gateway." Sacramento: California Higher Education Policy Center. ED 363 200. 35 pp. MF–01; PC–02.

Immerwahr, John, and James Harvey. 12 May 1995. "What the Public Thinks of Colleges." *Chronicle of Higher Education:* B1–B2.

Johnstone, Bruce. 1993. *Learning Productivity: A New Imperative for American Higher Education.* Albany: SUNY Press.

———. Autumn 1996. "Learning Productivity: Some Key Questions." *Learning Productivity News* 1: 1–3.

Jordan, Stephen M., and Daniel T. Layzell. November 1992. "A Case Study of Faculty Workload Issues in Arizona: Implications for State Higher Education Policy." Denver: State Higher Education Executive Officers. ED 356 729. 32 pp. MF–01; PC–02.

Kennedy, Donald. May/June 1995. "Another Century's End, Another Revolution for Higher Education." *Change* 27: 8–15.

Konrad, Alison M. Fall 1991. "Faculty Productivity and Demographics." *Thought and Action* 7: 19–54.

Konrad, Alison M., and Jeffrey Pfeffer. June 1990. "Do You Get What You Deserve? Factors Affecting the Relationship between Productivity and Pay." *Administrative Science Quarterly* 35: 258–85.

Kramon, G. 24 March 1991. "Medical Insurers Vary Fees to Aid Healthier People." *New York Times.*

Langenberg, D.N. 1992. "Marching to a Different Tune." *CGS Communicator* 25: 2–11.

Layzell, Daniel T. 19 February 1992. "Tight Budgets Demand Studies of Faculty Productivity." *Chronicle of Higher Education:* B1–B3.

Layzell, Daniel T., and J. Kent Caruthers. 1995. "Performance Funding at the State Level: Trends and Prospects." Paper presented at the 1995 Annual Meeting of the Association for the Study of Higher Education, November, Orlando, Florida. ED 391 406. 40 pp. MF–01; PC–02.

Layzell, Daniel T., Cheryl D. Lovell, and Judith I. Gill. 1996. "Developing Faculty as an Asset in a Period of Change and Uncertainty." In *Integrating Research on Faculty: Seeking New Ways to Communicate about the Academic Life of Faculty.* NCES 96-

---

849. Washington, D.C.: National Center for Education Statistics.

Leslie, Larry L., and Gary Rhoades. March/April 1995. "Rising Administrative Costs." *Journal of Higher Education* 66: 187–212.

Levin, Henry. Summer 1993. "Raising Productivity in Higher Education." *Higher Education Extension Service Review* 4: 1–11.

Lively, Kit. 24 February 1993. "States Step Up Efforts to End Remedial Courses at Four-Year Colleges." *Chronicle of Higher Education:* A28.

———. 23 February 1994. "Sabbaticals under Fire." *Chronicle of Higher Education:* A16.

Lovett, Clara M. 7 April 1995. "Breaking through Academic Gridlock." *Chronicle of Higher Education:* B1–B2.

Lunde, Joyce Povlacs, and Leverne A. Barrett. 1994. "Impact of an Intervention to Improve the Rewards for Teaching at a Research-Oriented University." Paper presented at the 1994 Annual Meeting of the American Educational Research Association, April 4–8, New Orleans, Louisiana. ED 372 667. 44 pp. MF–01; PC–02.

McGuinness, Aims D., Jr., and Peter T. Ewell. Fall 1994. "Improving Productivity and Quality in Higher Education." *AGB Priorities* 2: 1–12.

McNamee, Stephen J., and Cecil L. Willis. June 1994. "Stratification in Science." *Knowledge: Creation, Diffusion, Utilization* 15: 396–416.

Magner, Denise K. 13 September 1996a. "Fewer Professors Believe Western Culture Should Be the Cornerstone of the College Curriculum." *Chronicle of Higher Education:* A12–A15.

———. 12 April 1996b. "Professors' Salaries Hit $50,000, Edging Inflation." *Chronicle of Higher Education:* A18–A22.

Magrath, C. Peter. 28 February 1997. "Eliminating Tenure without Destroying Academic Freedom." *Chronicle of Higher Education:* A60.

Marchese, Ted. May/June 1995. "It's the System, Stupid." *Change* 27: 4.

Marien, Michael. May/June 1996. "Time to Rethink Knowledge Production and Higher Education." *On the Horizon* 4: 1–6.

Massy, William F. 1989. "Productivity Improvement Strategies for College and University Administration and Support Service." Paper presented at the Forum for College Financing, October 26, 1989, Annapolis, Maryland.

Massy, William F., and Andrea K. Wilger. 1992a. "New Fiscal Realities in Higher Education." *CPRE Finance Briefs:* 1–6.

———. Winter 1992b. "Productivity in Postsecondary Education: A New Approach." *Educational Evaluation and Policy Analysis* 14:

361–76.

———. July/August 1995. "Improving Productivity: What Faculty Think About It—and Its Effect on Quality." *Change* 27: 10–20.

———. January 1996. "It's Time to Redefine Quality." Paper presented at the AAHE Annual Conference on Faculty Roles and Rewards. Palo Alto, Calif.: Stanford Institute for Higher Education Research.

Massy, William, and Zemsky, Robert. September/October 1991. "Improving Academic Productivity: The New Frontier?" *Capital Ideas* 6: 1–14.

———. 1992. *Faculty Discretionary Time: Departments and the Academic Ratchet.* Philadelphia: Pew Higher Education Research Program.

———. January/February 1994. "Faculty Discretionary Time: Departments and the 'Academic Ratchet.'" *Journal of Higher Education* 65: 1–22.

———. 1995. *Using Information Technology to Enhance Academic Productivity.* Washington, D.C.: EDUCOM.

Mayhew, Lewis B., Patrick J. Ford, and Dean L. Hubbard. 1990. *The Quest for Quality: The Challenge for Undergraduate Education in the 1990s.* San Francisco: Jossey-Bass.

Metzler, Michael W. 1994. "Scholarship Reconsidered for the Professoriate of 2010." *Quest* 46: 440–55.

Middaugh, Michael F., and David E. Hollowell. Fall 1992. "Examining Academic and Productivity Measures." In *Containing Costs and Improving Productivity in Higher Education,* edited by Carol S. Hollins. New Directions for Institutional Research No. 75. San Francisco: Jossey-Bass.

Miles, Jack. November/December 1994. "A Modest Proposal for Saving University Research from the Budget Butcher." *Change* 26: 30–35.

Mingle, James R. 1992. "Faculty Work and the Cost/Quality/Access Collision." Denver: State Higher Education Executive Officers. ED 356 730. 17 pp. MF–01; PC–01.

Minnesota Higher Education Coordinating Board. January 1993. "Review and Comment on *Faculty Workload Report.*" St. Paul: Author.

Montana Office of the Legislative Auditor. December 1990. "Survey of University Staffing and Workloads." Report 90P-29. Helena: Author.

Murray, John P. Spring 1995. "The Teaching Portfolio: A Tool for Department Chairpersons to Create a Climate of Teaching Excellence." *Innovative Higher Education* 19: 163–75.

Myers, Michele Tolela. 7 June 1993. "Higher Education's Crisis of Imagination." *Higher Education & National Affairs* 42: 5–6.

National Center for Education Statistics. 1995. *Federal Support for Education: Fiscal Years 1980 to 1995.* Report No. NCES 95-215. Washington, D.C.: Author. ED 392 853. 51 pp. MF–01; PC–03.

———. July 1996. "Salaries of Full-Time Instructional Faculty, 1994–95." Washington, D.C.: Author. ED 397 528. 26 pp. MF–01; PC–02.

National Center for Higher Education Management Systems. 1993. "Engaging the Public in the Higher Education Debate." *NCHEMS News* 8: 2–3.

Nebraska Legislative Fiscal Office. July 1992. "University of Nebraska Workload Report to the Legislature." Lincoln: Author.

New York Office of the State Comptroller. April 1990. *State University of New York Faculty Utilization.* Report 90-S-89. Albany: Author. ED 344 563. 62 pp. MF–01; PC–03.

Nicklin, Julie L., and Goldie Blumenstyk. 6 January 1993. "Number of Nonteaching Staff Members Continues to Grow in Higher Education." *Chronicle of Higher Education:* A43–A44.

Noble, John H., Jr., Arthur G. Cryns, and Bertha S. Laury. June 1992. "Faculty Productivity and Costs: A Multivariate Analysis." *Evaluation Review* 16: 288–314.

Norris, Donald M. November/December 1996a. "Perpetual Learning as a Revolutionary Creation." *On the Horizon* 4: 1–6.

———. November/December 1996b. "Revolutionizing Strategy for the Knowledge Age." *On the Horizon* 4: 7–8.

Norris, William C., and Geraldine MacDonald. Fall 1993. "Evaluating the Increased Use of Technology in Instruction and Administration." In *Managing with Scarce Resources,* edited by William B. Simpson. New Directions for Institutional Research No. 79. San Francisco: Jossey-Bass.

O'Banion, Terry. June/July 1995. "School Is Out—Learning Is In." *On the Horizon* 3: 1–6.

———. December/January 1995–96. "A Learning College for the 21st Century." *Community College Journal* 66: 18–23.

Oberlin, John L. Spring 1996. "The Financial Mythology of Information Technology: The New Economics." *Cause/Effect* 19(1): 21–29.

Ohio Board of Regents. 1994. "Report of the Regents' Advisory Committee on Faculty Workload Standards and Guidelines." Columbus: Author.

Ohio Study Committee on Faculty Workload. 1992. "Report of the Study Committee on Faculty Workload." Columbus: Author.

Olson, Jeffrey E. October 1994. "Institutional and Technical Con-
straints on Faculty Gross Productivity in American Doctoral
Universities." *Research in Higher Education* 35: 549–67.

Oregon State System of Higher Education. 24 January 1997. "Faculty Work and Results." Eugene: Author.

Pascarella, Ernest T., and Patrick T. Terenzini. 1991. *How College
Affects Students.* San Francisco: Jossey-Bass.

Pew Higher Education Research Program. September 1991. "An
End to Sanctuary." *Policy Perspectives* 3: 1A–8A.

———. March 1992a. "Keeping the Promise." *Policy Perspectives* 4:
1A–8A.

———. September 1992b. "Testimony from the Belly of the
Whale." *Policy Perspectives* 4: 1A–8A.

———. April 1994. "To Dance with Change." *Policy Perspectives* 5:
1A–12A.

———. April 1995. "Twice Imagined." *Policy Perspectives* 6:
1A–11A.

———. November 1996a. "Rumblings." *Policy Perspectives* 7: 1–10.
ED 404 894. 14 pp. MF–01; PC–01.

———. April 1996b. "Shared Purposes." *Policy Perspectives* 6: 1–10.
ED 395 558. 14 pp. MF–01; PC not available EDRS.

Pickens, William H. Fall 1993. "Measures of Resource Scarcity in
Higher Education." In *Managing with Scarce Resources,* edited
by William B. Simpson. New Directions for Institutional Research No. 79. San Francisco: Jossey-Bass.

———. May 1995. *Financing the Plan: California's Master Plan for
Higher Education, 1960 to 1994.* Sacramento: California Higher
Education Policy Center. ED 399 849. 64 pp. MF–01; PC–03.

Plater, William M. May/June 1995. "Future Work: Faculty Time in
the 21st Century." *Change* 27: 22–33.

President's Council of Advisors on Science and Technology. 1992.
*Renewing the Promise: Research-Intensive Universities and the
Nation.* Washington, D.C.: Author. ED 353 946. 69 pp. MF–01;
PC–03.

Research Associates of Washington. 1995. *Inflation Measures for
Schools, Colleges, and Libraries: 1995 Update.* Washington, D.C.:
Author.

———. 1996. *State Profiles: Financing Public Higher Education,
1996 Rankings.* Washington, D.C: Author.

Rhode Island Office of the Auditor General. November 1986. *A
Review of "University of Rhode Island Faculty Workload."* Cran-
ston: Author.

Rice, R. Eugene. 1996. *Making a Place for the New American*

Scholar. Washington, D.C.: American Association for Higher Education.

Rodriguez, Esther M., and Sandra S. Ruppert. October 1996. "Postsecondary Education and the New Workforce." Denver: State Higher Education Executive Officers. ED 401 845. 33 pp. MF–01; PC–02.

Rosovsky, Henry. 1990. *The University: An Owners' Manual.* New York: W.W. Norton & Co.

Roush, C. 24 March 1991. "Small Employers Ill over Health Benefits." *Tampa Tribune.*

Ruppert, Sandra S. 1996. *The Politics of Remedy: State Legislative Views on Higher Education.* Washington, D.C.: National Education Association. ED 391 445. 61 pp. MF–01; PC not available EDRS.

Russell, Alene. 1992. "Report on Faculty Workload." Denver: State Higher Education Executive Officers.

Sadowski, Cyril J., and Allen K. Hess. February 1994. "A Modified Accomplishment Record Approach to Evaluating Teaching Effectiveness under the Talent Development Model." *Journal of Personnel Evaluation in Education* 8: 41–46.

Schaefer, William D. 1990. *Education without Compromise: From Chaos to Coherence in Higher Education.* San Francisco: Jossey-Bass.

Schomberg, Steven F., and James A. Farmer, Jr. Fall 1994. "The Evolving Concept of Public Service and Implications for Rewarding Faculty." *Continuing Higher Education Review* 58: 122–40.

Scott, Robert A. 26 July 1993. "Student Learning: The Priority for the Future." *Higher Education and National Affairs* 42: 5.

Scott, Robert K., and Susan M. Awbrey. July/August 1993. "Transforming Scholarship." *Change* 25: 38–43.

Smith, Kathleen S., and Ronald D. Simpson. Spring 1995. "Validating Teacher Competencies for Faculty Members in Higher Education: A National Study Using the Delphi Method." *Innovative Higher Education* 19: 223–34.

Smith, Peter. 1990. *Killing the Spirit: Higher Education in America.* New York: Penguin Books.

Social Science Research Center. 30 May 1990. *CSU Faculty Workload Study.* Fullerton, Calif.: Author. ED 348 917. 367 pp. MF–01; PC–15.

South Dakota Board of Regents. May 1994. "HERI 1993 Faculty Survey." Pierre: Author.

Stanford Forum for Higher Education Futures. 1995. *Leveraged*

Learning: Technology's Role in Restructuring Higher Education.
Stanford, Calif.: Author.

State College and University Systems of West Virginia. 1993. "Statement on Faculty Workload." *Administrative Bulletin* 26. Charles-
ton: Author.

State Council of Higher Education for Virginia. June 1991. "An
Overview of Results from the Virginia Faculty Survey." Roanoke:
Author.

State University of New York and California State University Faculty
Senates. March 1997. "Public Higher Education and Productivity:
A Faculty Voice." Albany/Sacramento: Author.

Sykes, Charles J. 1988. *ProfScam.* New York: St. Martin's Press.

Texas Higher Education Coordinating Board. June 1993. *Faculty
Teaching Workload in Texas Public Universities, 1983–1992.*
Austin: Author.

Texas Office of the State Auditor. May 1994. *Faculty Workload
Policies and the Use of Faculty Teaching Resources at Four
Research Universities.* Report No. 94-117. Austin: Author.

TIAA-CREF. 1990. *College and University Employee Retirement and
Insurance Benefits Cost Survey.* New York: Teachers Insurance
and Annuity Association. ED 364 155. 70 pp. MF–01; PC–03.

U.S. Bureau of the Census. 1995. *Statistical Abstract: 1995.* Washington, D.C.: Author.

U.S. Department of Education. 1990. *Faculty in Higher Education
Institutions, 1988.* Report No. NCES 90-365. Washington, D.C.:
Author. ED 321 628. 209 pp. MF–01; PC–09.

———. 1991. *Profiles of Faculty in Higher Education Institutions,
1988.* Report No. NCES 91-389. Washington, D.C.: National
Center for Education Statistics.

———. 1993. "Time to Complete Baccalaureate Degree." *Indicator
of the Month.* Report No. NCES 93-641. Washington, D.C.: National Center for Education Statistics.

———. 1995. *Digest of Education Statistics, 1995.* Report No. NCES
95-029. Washington, D.C.: National Center for Education Statistics. ED 387 885. 604 pp. MF–03; PC–25.

———. 1996a. *Institutional Policies and Practices Regarding Faculty
in Higher Education.* Report No. NCES 97-080. Washington, D.C.:
National Center for Education Statistics. ED 402 858. 111 pp.
MF–01; PC 05.

———. 1996b. "Salaries of Full-Time Instructional Faculty, 1994–
95." Report No. NCES 96-855. Washington, D.C.: National Center
for Education Statistics. ED 397 528. 26 pp. MF–01; PC–02.

———. 1997. *Advanced Telecommunications in U.S. Public Ele-*

mentary and Secondary Schools, Fall 1996. Report No. NCES 97-944. Washington, D.C.: National Center for Education Statistics.

Vamos, Mark N. 11 March 1996. "America, Land of the Shaken." *Business Week:* 64–65.

Wadsworth, Deborah. June 1995. "The New Public Landscape." *AAHE Bulletin* 48: 14–17.

Waggaman, John S. 1991. *Strategies and Consequences: Managing the Costs in Higher Education.* ASHE-ERIC Higher Education Report No. 8. Washington, D.C.: George Washington Univ., Graduate School of Education and Human Development. ED 347 921. 148 pp. MF–01; PC–06.

Washington Higher Education Coordinating Board. 1994. *Faculty Workload Study.* Olympia: Author.

Washington Office of the Forecast Council. 1996. "Washington Economic and Revenue Forecast." Olympia: Author.

Western Interstate Commission for Higher Education. 1993. *High School Graduates: Projections by State, 1992–2009.* Boulder, Colo.: Author.

Wheatley, Margaret J. 1992. *Leadership and the New Science.* San Francisco: Berrett-Koehler.

Wilson, Ian. March/April 1996. "The Practical Power of Vision." *On the Horizon* 4: 1–5.

Wilson, Robin. 28 February 1997. "Faculty Leaders in N.Y. and California Unite on Productivity Issues." *Chronicle of Higher Education:* A12.

Wingspread Group on Higher Education. 1993. *An American Imperative: Higher Expectations for Higher Education.* Racine, Wisc.: Johnson Foundation. ED 364 144. 177 pp. MF–01; PC–08.

Wisconsin Legislative Audit Bureau. June 1993. "Teaching Loads within the University of Wisconsin System." Report 93-15. Madison: Author.

Yuker, Harold E. 1984. *Faculty Workload: Research, Theory, and Interpretation.* ASHE-ERIC Higher Education Report No. 10. Washington, D.C.: Association for the Study of Higher Education. ED 259 691. 120 pp. MF–01; PC–05.

Zemsky, Robert. 1996. "The Impact of Higher Education's New Climate on Faculty Perceptions." In *Integrating Research on Faculty: Seeking New Ways to Communicate about the Academic Life of Faculty.* Report No. NCES 96-849. Washington, D.C.: National Center for Education Statistics.

Zemsky, Robert, and William F. Massy. November/December 1990. "Cost Containment." *Change* 22: 16–22.

———. November/December 1995. "Toward an Understanding of

Our Current Predicaments." *Change* 27: 41–49.

Zemsky, Robert, William F. Massy, and P. Oedel. May/June 1993. "On Reversing the Ratchet." *Change* 23: 56–62.

INDEX

A

academic avoidance of change, 59
academic freedom redefinition, 76
"academic ratchet," 11–12
       pursuit of research enabled through, 12
accountability reporting on higher education required by states, 31
accreditation
       perception that will protect higher education from
          competition being abandoned, 72
"accretion of unnecessary tasks," 11
"administrative lattice," 11
administrators increasingly in role of messenger who gets shot, 60
Alaska
       accountability reporting on higher education required by, 31
An American Imperative
       on mismatch between what Americans need and what they
          are getting from higher education, 29–30
Arizona
       accountability reporting on higher education required by, 31
       annotated bibliography of faculty workload studies in, 85
       average weekly classroom hours in, 41
       limits growth in appropriations, 19
       mandate to report Faculty Workload, 47
       performance based funding for higher education system, 32
Arkansas
       accountability reporting on higher education required by, 31
       considered reducing remediation courses, 26
       performance-based funding for higher education intended
          by, 32
"autopoetic" fashion
       system change in an, 82
average income in 1995–96 of faculty, 7–8
average weekly classroom hours, 41
awards for research and teaching realignment, 73–76

B

baby boom echo, 1
beliefs as barriers to solutions, 53–60
Boggs (1995–96) study of learning paradigm, 62
budget increase compared with the previous year, 1991–1995, 25
budgeting should be decentralized to the operational unit, 76–77
budget squeeze, 20–25
business view of higher education, 29–30

C

D

"dangerous mismatch." *See An American Imperative.*
decisions
    institutions need ability to make, 81–82
Democrats think funding for higher education not adequate, 31
DePaul University decline in faculty workload devoted to
  teaching and preparing courses over time, 41–42
"destructuring the curriculum" result, 12
Diamond, Robert, 80
doctoral programs
    recent emphasis on pedagogy in, 15
Duke University, 13

E

education system more organized to discourage than to cultivate
  and support students, 26
Ewell (1994b) best captured type of miscommunication between
  outsiders and insiders in higher education, 37
expenditures in higher education
    measures of price changes for, 10
experimentation required for restructuring, 78

F

faculty
    activity outcomes, 66
    fallacy of autonomous faculty, 56
    average income in 1995–96, 7–8
    characterizing productivity, 51
    community must accept ownership for health of institutions
     and cooperate in curing them, 79
    productivity definitions, 48
    stake in positive consequences of reallocation, 77
    role increasingly defined in terms of ability to facilitate
     student learning, 64
    total hours per week spent in all activities, 41
    workload definitions, 39–40
faculty effort focus of states because portion of budget most likely
  to reap immediate benefits, 26
faculty workload studies
    annotated bibliography, 85–86
    genesis of, 26
    limitation on, ix

push for, 38
questions that need to be asked in preparing, ix
reasons for, ix
faltering economic factors, 4–75
family payment effort
national trends, 27
tuition as a percent of median household income, 26
Federal spending on postsecondary education decline, 23
financial assistance
required for increasing numbers of college population, 3–4
"fitness-for-use" criteria, 65
Florida
accountability reporting on higher education required by, 31
legislature passed the 12-hour rule, 46
limit on increases in property taxes, 19
mandate from state legislature to report faculty workload, 47
performance-based funding for higher education intended
by, 32
"function lust," 11

G

Gann initiative, 19
Gardner, David, 80
general fund budget increases, nominal and real, 1980 to 1994, 21
Georgia accountability reporting on higher education, 31
"Golden Fleece" award, 16
guides for improving productivity, 77

H

Harvard University, 13
Harvey (1995) on public expectations and thoughts of higher
education, 32
Harvey and Associates (1994) on public expectations and thoughts
of higher education, 32
Harvey and Immerwahr (1995a, 1995b) on public expectations and
thoughts of higher education, 32
Hawaii accountability reporting on higher education, 31
Headlee Amendment, 19
HEPI. *See* higher education price index.
higher education
external constituents ask different questions, 38
funding as percent of state general fund from 1990 to 1993, 20
how it views its world, 36–38

how legislatures view, 30–32
price index
growth in, 7
how legislatures view higher education, 30–32

I

IBM Global Campus, 58
Idaho
    accountability reporting on higher education required by, 31
    annotated bibliography of faculty workload studies in, 85
    performance-based funding for higher education intended
        by, 32
Illinois
    accountability reporting on higher education required by, 31
    annotated bibliography of faculty workload studies in, 85
    state with mandate from higher education authority
        to report faculty workload, 47
imagination
    crisis in higher education of, 77–78
increased costs
    how they have been covered, 16–18
incremental change problem, 78–79
Indiana
    accountability reporting on higher education required by, 31
    mandate from state legislature to report faculty workload, 47
information services
    great increase in demand, 8–9
institutional need to provide competitive services, 73
institutions should embrace a mission rather than be all things to
    all people, 67
instruction percent effort, 42
insufficient learning culprits, 62–63
Internet
growth in use, 72
"invisible college," 49
Iowa higher education authority mandate to report faculty
    workload, 47

K

Kansas accountability reporting on higher education, 31
Kennedy, Donald, 80
Kentucky
    accountability reporting on higher education required by, 31

Massy and Zemsky (1992) on role of proliferation of courses and increasing specialization, 12

measurement of learning problems, 55

Michigan

    accountability reporting on higher education required by, 31

    Headlee Amendment, 19

    higher education funding as a percent of state general fund did not fall from 1990 to 1993, 20

Minnesota

    accountability reporting on higher education required by, 31

    annotated bibliography of faculty workload studies in, 85

    average weekly classroom hours in, 41

    performance-based funding for higher education intended by, 32

    mandate from state legislature to report faculty workload, 47

minority population increase in college population, 3

miscommunication between academics and legislators, 37

"mission confusion" contribution to increased costs, 14–16

Mississippi higher education authority

    order to report faculty workload, 47

Missouri

    accountability reporting on higher education required by, 31

    performance-based funding for higher education intended by, 32

Montana

    annotated bibliography of faculty workload studies in, 85

    percent effort on instruction in, 42

N

NALS. *See* National Adult Literacy Survey.

National Adult Literacy Survey of 1993, 29

National Center for Higher Education Management Systems

    concerns with student access to specific required courses, 31

    design national database with common definitions of terms, 40

National Conference of State Legislatures, 30

national learning infrastructure

lack of, 65

national norms for percent of faculty effort, 44–45

NCHEMS. *See* National Center for Higher Education Management Systems.

Nebraska

    annotated bibliography of faculty workload studies in, 85

limits on property taxes, 19

performance-based funding for higher education intended
by, 32

undertook studies to assess remedial education, 26

Nevada 1996 tax measures, 20

New Jersey accountability reporting on higher education, 31

New Mexico

accountability reporting on higher education required by, 31

mandate from state legislature to report faculty workload, 47

New York

accountability reporting on higher education required by, 31

annotated bibliography of faculty workload studies in,
85–86

performance-based funding for higher education approaches
under discussion or partially implemented by, 32

New York City and State considered raising entry requirements, 26

nontraditional students increasing part of college population, 4

North Carolina

accountability reporting on higher education required by, 31

performance-based funding for higher education approaches
under discussion or partially implemented by, 32

O

O'Banion (1995–96) study of learning paradigm, 62

Ohio

accountability reporting on higher education required by, 31

annotated bibliography of faculty workload studies in, 86

legislature ordered 10 percent increase in undergraduate
teaching, 46

mandate from state legislature to report faculty workload, 47

performance-based funding for higher education intended
by, 32

Oklahoma

considered raising entry requirements, 26

1996 tax measures, 20

Oregon

annotated bibliography of faculty workload studies in, 86

limits to state spending, 20

mandate from higher education authority to report faculty
workload, 47

"output creep," 11, 14

outputs

importance of higher education defining, 65–66

P

Pascarella and Terenzini (1991)

    compilation of extant research on outcomes of college, 65–66

Pennsylvania legislature mandate to report faculty workload, 47

perceptions role, 29–38

performance-based funding, 66

    for higher education system intended by 14 states, 32

personal computer increase in use, 72

population pressure

    growth in, 1–4

prestige

    defined as ability to attract resources, 13

    not the same as quality, 13

productive learning conditions, 63

productivity problem, 25–28

productivity and workload should not be confused, 48

Proposition 13 limiting property taxes in California, 19

Proposition 98, 19

public criticism of faculty workloads

    attributed to misunderstandings by "outsiders," 36

public views of higher education, 32–35

"publish or perish," 14

pursuit of research enabled through "academic ratchet," 12

Q

quality

    successful fulfillment of an institution's mission, 13

questions that need to be asked in preparing faculty workload
  studies, ix

R

Republicans think funding for higher education is adequate, 31

research

    in future, 75

    negatively correlated with "student orientation," 14

    productivity, 48

research by institutional mission

    percent of time spent on, 44

retirement uncapping role in increasing costs, 12

Rhode Island

    accountability reporting on higher education required by, 31

    mandate from higher education authority to report faculty
      workload, 47

percent effort on instruction in, 42
rising tuition important concern of public, 33
role of
>proliferation of courses and increasing specialization, 12
>sabbaticals role in increasing costs, 12
>tenure in increasing costs, 12

S

"scholarly drivel," 16
scholarly pursuits redefinition, 74
scholarship of engagement, 74
service
>need for way to assess productivity as it relates to, 50
seven principles of good practice
>technology can be used to implement, 69
SHEEO. *See* State Higher Education Executive Officers.
social science faculty have consistent relationships between
>number of publications and instructor's effectiveness, 49
South Carolina
>accountability reporting on higher education required by, 31
>annotated bibliography of faculty workload studies in, 86
>cuts in property taxes, 19
>mandate from state legislature to report faculty workload, 47
>performance-based funding for higher education intended
>>by, 32
South Dakota
>annotated bibliography of faculty workload studies in, 86
>1996 tax measures, 20
spending from general fund on higher education falling, 20–21
Stanford University, 80
state
>spending by major program area percent change, 22
>spending increases, 1991 to 1993, 21
>willingness to spend on higher education importance, 23
State Higher Education Executive Officers
>found 21 states had mandated faculty workload minimum
>>or reporting of it, 46–47
"sticky" production function, 54
strategic investment plans for technology need, 71
student learning focus, 62–65
"student orientation"
>factors that correlate with, 14–15
"subversive" strategy with ability to question assumptions, 80

SUNY percent effort on instruction, 42
Syracuse University, 80
system change in an "autopoetic" fashion, 82

T
taxpayers' revolt, 18–20
teaching
      paradigm fallacy, 53–54
      portfolio, 50
      productivity has little literature or methodology, 50
      time negatively related to salary, 15
teaching by institutional mission and faculty rank
      percent of time spent on, 43
technology
      helping higher education increase its productivity, 70
      making possible an unprecedented growth in education, 71
      may mean faculty will teach less in the traditional manner, 69
      need to realize the potential of, 68–71
Tennessee
      accountability reporting on higher education required by, 32
      considered reducing remediation courses, 26
      performance-based funding for higher education intended
          by, 32
Texas
      accountability reporting on higher education required by, 32
      annotated bibliography of faculty workload studies in, 86
      considered raising entry requirements, 26
      mandate from state legislature to report faculty workload, 47
      performance-based funding for higher education intended
          by, 32
      tied state spending increases to personal income growth, 19
threefold necessary restructuring, 77
Tidal Wave II. *See* baby boom echo.
time spent as approximation of learning, 56
"tough love" for higher education, 36
tuition increases from 1991–1995, 17
12-hour rule, 46

U
undergraduate population in California
      suggestions for handling increasing, 2
University and Community College System of Nevada, ix
University of California, 80

University of Chicago, 13
University of Delaware costs, 11–12
University of Michigan, 80
U.S. Department of Education list
       average weekly classroom hours in, 41
       percent effort on instruction of, 42
Utah
       accountability reporting on higher education required by, 32
       mandate from state legislature to report faculty workload, 47

V

Virginia
       accountability reporting on higher education required by, 32
       annotated bibliography of faculty workload studies in, 86
       average weekly classroom hours in, 41
       considered raising entry requirements, 26
"visionary leadership" needed in higher education, 80–81

W

"warranty" program for West Virginia high schools, 25–26
Washington
       accountability reporting on higher education required by, 32
       annotated bibliography of faculty workload studies in, 86
       average weekly classroom hours in, 41
       performance-based funding for higher education, 32
       mandate from state legislature to report faculty workload, 47
       undertook studies to assess extent of remedial education, 26
Washington State Initiative 601, 20
"wastage" in higher education unacceptable in private sector, 25
"weeding" high cost, 26
Western Governors University, 58
Western Interstate Commission for Higher Education, 1
West Virginia
       accountability reporting on higher education required by, 32
       legislature demanded faculty productivity exceed average
         faculty productivity by 10 percent, 46
       mandate from state legislature to report faculty workload, 47
       "warranty" program considered for high schools, 25–26
WICHE. *See* Western Interstate Commission for Higher Education.
Wingspread Group (1993) refers to high cost of "weeding," 26
Wisconsin
       accountability reporting on higher education required by, 32
       annotated bibliography of faculty workload studies in, 86

mandate from higher education authority to report faculty workload, 47
workload and productivity
    problems with using concepts, 51–52
    should not be confused, 48

Z

Zemsky practitioner of "tough love" for higher education, 36

ASHE-ERIC HIGHER EDUCATION REPORTS

Since 1983, the Association for the Study of Higher Education (ASHE) and the Educational Resources Information Center (ERIC) Clearinghouse on Higher Education, a sponsored project of the Graduate School of Education and Human Development at The George Washington University, have cosponsored the ASHE-ERIC Higher Education Report series. This volume is the twenty-sixth overall and the ninth to be published by the Graduate School of Education and Human Development at The George Washington University.

Each monograph is the definitive analysis of a tough higher education problem, based on thorough research of pertinent literature and institutional experiences. Topics are identified by a national survey. Noted practitioners and scholars are then commissioned to write the reports, with experts providing critical reviews of each manuscript before publication.

Eight monographs (10 before 1985) in the ASHE-ERIC Higher Education Report series are published each year and are available on individual and subscription bases. To order, use the order form on the last page of this book.

Qualified persons interested in writing a monograph for the ASHE-ERIC Higher Education Report series are invited to submit a proposal to the National Advisory Board. As the preeminent literature review and issue analysis series in higher education, the Higher Education Reports are guaranteed wide dissemination and national exposure for accepted candidates. Execution of a monograph requires at least a minimal familiarity with the ERIC database, including *Resources in Education* and the current *Index to Journals in Education*. The objective of these reports is to bridge conventional wisdom with practical research. Prospective authors are strongly encouraged to call Dr. Fife at (800) 773-3742.

For further information, write to
ASHE-ERIC Higher Education Reports Series
The George Washington University
One Dupont Circle, Suite 630
Washington, DC 20036
Or phone (202) 296-2597 ext. 13; toll free: (800) 773-ERIC ext. 13.

Write or call for a complete catalog.

Visit our Web site at **www.gwu.edu/~eriche/Reports**

ADVISORY BOARD

James Earl Davis
University of Delaware at Newark

Kenneth A. Feldman
State University of New York–Stony Brook

Kassie Freeman
Peabody College, Vanderbilt University

Susan Frost
Emory University

Kenneth P. Gonzalez
Arizona State University

Esther E. Gotlieb
West Virginia University

Philo Hutcheson
Georgia State University

Laurence R. Marcus
Rowan College

Robert Menges
Northwestern University

Diane E. Morrison
Centre for Curriculum, Transfer, and Technology

L. Jackson Newell
University of Utah

Steven G. Olswang
University of Washington

Laura W. Perna
Frederick D. Patterson Research
  Institute of the College Fund/UNCF

R. Eugene Rice
American Association for Higher Education

Brent Ruben
State University of New Jersey–Rutgers

Sherry Sayles-Folks
Eastern Michigan University

Jack H. Schuster
Claremont Graduate School—Center for Educational Studies

Daniel Seymour
Claremont College–California

Marilla D. Svinicki
University of Texas–Austin

David Sweet
OERI, U.S. Department of Education

Jon E. Travis
Texas A & M University

Gershon Vincow
Syracuse University

Dan W. Wheeler
University of Nebraska–Lincoln

Donald H. Wulff
University of Washington

Manta Yorke
Liverpool John Moores University

REVIEW PANEL

Richard Alfred
University of Michigan

Robert J. Barak
Iowa State Board of Regents

Alan Bayer
Virginia Polytechnic Institute and State University

John P. Bean
Indiana University–Bloomington

John M. Braxton
Peabody College, Vanderbilt University

Ellen M. Brier
Tennessee State University

Dennis Brown
University of Kansas

Patricia Carter
University of Michigan

John A. Centra
Syracuse University

Paul B. Chewning
Council for the Advancement and Support of Education

Arthur W. Chickering
Vermont College

Darrel A. Clowes
Virginia Polytechnic Institute and State University

Deborah M. DiCroce
Piedmont Virginia Community College

Dorothy E. Finnegan
The College of William & Mary

Kenneth C. Green
Claremont Graduate University

James C. Hearn
University of Georgia

Edward R. Hines
Illinois State University

Deborah Hunter
University of Vermont

Linda K. Johnsrud
University of Hawaii at Manoa

Bruce Anthony Jones
University of Missouri–Columbia

Elizabeth A. Jones
West Virginia University

Marsha V. Krotseng
State College and University Systems of West Virginia

George D. Kuh
Indiana University–Bloomington

J. Roderick Lauver
Planned Systems International, Inc.–Maryland

Daniel T. Layzell
MGT of America–Wisconsin

Patrick G. Love
Kent State University

Meredith Jane Ludwig
Education Statistics Services Institute

Mantha V. Mehallis
Florida Atlantic University

Toby Milton
Essex Community College

John A. Muffo
Virginia Polytechnic Institute and State University

Kathryn Nemeth Tuttle
University of Kansas

L. Jackson Newell
Deep Springs College

Mark Oromaner
Hudson Community College

James C. Palmer
Illinois State University

Robert A. Rhoads
Michigan State University

G. Jeremiah Ryan
Quincy College

Mary Ann Danowitz Sagaria
The Ohio State University

RECENT TITLES

Volume 25 ASHE-ERIC Higher Education Reports

1. A Culture for Academic Excellence: Implementing the Quality Principles in Higher Education
   Jann E. Freed, Marie R. Klugman, and Jonathan D. Fife

2. From Discipline to Development: Rethinking Student Conduct in Higher Education
   Michael Dannells

3. Academic Controversy: Enriching College Instruction through Intellectual Conflict
   David W. Johnson, Roger T. Johnson, and Karl A. Smith

4. Higher Education Leadership: Analyzing the Gender Gap
   Luba Chliwniak

5. The Virtual Campus: Technology and Reform in Higher Education
   Gerald C. Van Dusen

6. Early Intervention Programs: Opening the Door to Higher Education
   Robert H. Fenske, Christine A. Geranios, Jonathan E. Keller, and David E. Moore

7. The Vitality of Senior Faculty Members: Snow on the Roof—Fire in the Furnace
   Carole J. Bland and William H. Bergquist

8. A National Review of Scholastic Achievement in General Education: How Are We Doing and Why Should We Care?
   Steven J. Osterlind

Volume 24 ASHE-ERIC Higher Education Reports

1. Tenure, Promotion, and Reappointment: Legal and Administrative Implications (951)
   Benjamin Baez and John A. Centra

2. Taking Teaching Seriously: Meeting the Challenge of Instructional Improvement (952)
   Michael B. Paulsen and Kenneth A. Feldman

3. Empowering the Faculty: Mentoring Redirected and Renewed (953)
   Gaye Luna and Deborah L. Cullen

4. Enhancing Student Learning: Intellectual, Social, and Emotional Integration (954)
   Anne Goodsell Love and Patrick G. Love

5. Benchmarking in Higher Education: Adapting Best Practices to Improve Quality (955)
   Jeffrey W. Alstete

6. Models for Improving College Teaching: A Faculty Resource (956)
   Jon E. Travis